Practical
Strategies
for *Successful*
Classrooms

Instructional Strategies for Diverse Learners

Wendy Conklin, M.A.

SHELL EDUCATION

Instructional Strategies for Diverse Learners

Editor
Maria Elvira Kessler, M.A.

Project Manager
Maria Elvira Kessler, M.A.

Editor-in-Chief
Sharon Coan, M.S.Ed.

Creative Director
Lee Aucoin

Cover Design
Lee Aucoin
Lesley Palmer

Imaging
Phil Garcia

Lead Print Designer
Don Tran

Publisher
Corinne Burton, M.A.Ed.

Shell Education
5301 Oceanus Drive
Huntington Beach, CA 92649-1030

www.shelleducation.com

ISBN-1-4258-0373-3

© 2006 Shell Education

Reprinted, 2007

Made in U.S.A.

Table of Contents

Table of Contents *(cont.)*

Introduction

There are many teaching strategies in the education world today. Some enhance learning and some do not. This book details eight different kinds of strategies that enhance learning. With the demanding needs of diverse students in our schools today, the necessity for making the curriculum accessible to everyone is central to successfully teaching all students. Teachers need strategies that enhance learning for everyone. The strategies in this book enhance learning in a way that can also differentiate the curriculum for diverse learners. This book defines each strategy, shows why each should be used, and gives ideas for their use.

Within this book you will find:

- A vocabulary review and glossary of relevant terminology

- Pre-reading reflections and other opportunities to reflect—these give the learner an opportunity to activate prior learning and apply the skills of a reflective practitioner

- Chapter reviews at the end of each chapter to check newly-acquired knowledge

- References of professional readings for the analysis of new information and reflection

- Direct instruction/information that provides information applicable to the topic

- Application opportunities for the learner to reinforce the content

Each chapter in this book covers a different strategy that enhances learning. **Chapter 1** explains what brainstorming is and why it should be used in the classroom. Graphic organizers are covered in **Chapter 2** to show how they formulate patterns in much the same way that the brain seeks out patterns. **Chapter 3** explains several different types of questioning techniques and how to recognize good questions. A set of steps is provided in **Chapter 4** to show how a teacher can implement problem-based learning. **Chapter 5** explores the value of primary sources. In **Chapter 6**, different kinds of simulations are shown. The theory of multiple intelligences, as well as practical ways to implement the theory, is explored in **Chapter 7**. Finally, the unusual concept of using creative dramatics in the classroom is studied in **Chapter 8**.

Vocabulary Review

Education is notorious for its jargon. Many specific terms that are used in this book are provided here. Before you begin reading, note your initial definition of each term. Then, when you have finished reading the book, note your final definition of each term. You will also find the definitions of these terms in the Glossary.

Term	My First Definition	My Final Definition
active learners		
Attribute Listing Method		
authentic learning		
Bloom's Taxonomy		
brainstorming		
brainwriting		
complexity		
creative dramatics		
curiosity		
differentiation		

Term	My First Definition	My Final Definition
elaboration		
electronic brainstorming		
flexibility		
fluency		
graphic organizer		
imagination		
lateral thinking		
Morphological Synthesis		
Multiple Intelligences Theory		
originality		
passive learners		
primary sources		

Term	My First Definition	My Final Definition
problem-based learning		
problem statement		
reverse brainstorming		
risk taking		
SCAMPER		
semantic memories		
simulations		
Socratic Seminar		
Three Story Intellect Model		
vertical thinking		
visual learners		
Williams' Taxonomy		

Chapter 1 Pre-Reading Reflection

1. What are some ways to get your students to be creative thinkers?

   _____

   _____

   _____

   _____

2. Why should teachers have their students brainstorm?

   _____

   _____

   _____

   _____

3. What are some basic rules that teachers should enforce when having their students brainstorm in their classroom?

   _____

   _____

   _____

   _____

Brainstorming

Businesses use it all the time to develop new products, to improve existing products, and to solve marketing and advertising problems. Teachers use it to compel students to be creative and to solve real-life problems in the classroom.

Getting students to generate new ideas can be a difficult task, even for the best teacher. Many students are afraid of letting others know about their ideas for fear of criticism. How can teachers get the creative juices flowing in their classrooms on a daily basis? One of the best ways is by teaching students how to brainstorm effectively.

Brainstorming is a method of thinking up new concepts, ideas, or solutions. Take the word *brainstorm* and separate the two words, *brain* and *storm*. To brainstorm means to use the *brain* to *storm* (or think of) creative problems. Alex Osborn, the advertising executive who is affectionately named the father of brainstorming, coined the word *brainstorm* back in 1939. He said that *storm* meant to take charge as "in commando fashion, each stormer audaciously attacking the same objective" (1953, p. 297). Osborn believed that creative ideas should be expressed without any judgment or evaluation. He did not believe that one could be both creative and critical at the same time. Some of the ideas produced in a brainstorming session will be wild and crazy. Oftentimes, these ideas lead to the best solutions. Osborn said, "It is easier to tone down a wild idea than to think up a new one" (Davis, 1998, p. 174).

Brainstorming is a type of lateral thinking. Edward de Bono, a psychologist and professor of investigative medicine at Cambridge University, coined the term *lateral thinking*. *Vertical thinking* occurs when one solves a problem by going from one logical step to another logical step (De Bono, 1970). Lateral thinking comes from seeking solutions to problems through unconventional methods, as illustrated in Figure 1.1.

Figure 1.1: Lateral vs. Vertical Thinking

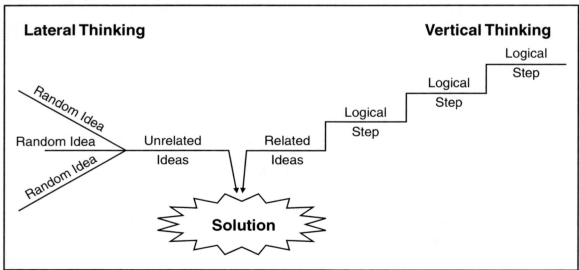

Our brains function very differently than computers. It takes years before we learn to do simple math problems, but it takes computers only seconds. The brain is a patterned recognition system, and we quickly and easily recognize faces, languages, and objects. It is easy to get stuck in our patterned way of thinking, but lateral thinking helps us to break out of this habit. Lateral thinking generates new ideas and concepts. Brainstorming helps students to break out of their patterned way of thinking and look at things in a new way.

Why Use Brainstorming?

Brainstorming strengthens a person's natural abilities, which improves both teamwork and productivity. Many believe that creativity is the most important human resource of all. Without creativity, we would see no progress and would be perpetually repeating the same patterns.

To understand the benefits of brainstorming, it might help to look at why so many businesses utilize it. Businesses use it with their employees to help produce creative solutions to problems. Someday many of your students will be called on in the workplace for creative ideas. Will they be able to meet the task? One thing we know is that those who are able to brainstorm will be able to solve problems more efficiently.

The main reason many people like brainstorming is because it generates so many ideas in a short amount of time. Whether it is a company looking for a new advertising campaign for a product or a classroom trying to decide how to raise money for charity, many ideas can be generated in just a matter of minutes.

It is important to know that creative thinking is a skill that can be taught and learned. Brainstorming increases mental capacity to think creatively, which improves with practice. The more we practice thinking creatively, the more creatively we will think. It's a skill that can be used with any age group or learning level.

Creatively thinking individuals can see the best ideas when they arise. Many times these ideas are the crazy ones, but if seen in a creative light, they become the appropriate choices for the occasion. For example, how can a company keep from being bought out by a competitor? By giving things away for free! This very idea kept a software company from being taken over by Microsoft.

How to Implement Brainstorming

When brainstorming is done correctly, it taps into the brain's capacity for creative thinking. There are many ways a teacher can implement the brainstorming technique in the classroom. If the class has many students, divide it into small groups where students will feel more at ease. Another alternative is to have each student brainstorm an individual list and then share it with the class. Oftentimes, using individual brainstorming sessions can be just as productive.

To ensure a productive brainstorming session, here are some general guidelines:

1. Before getting started, formulate an open-ended question for students to brainstorm. It should not be too specific or have just one right answer. This question should be shared the day before the brainstorming session so that students can be thinking about it ahead of time.

2. Set aside a specific time for brainstorming. Brainstorming sessions should not last very long—five to 15 minutes should be enough time in the classroom.

3. No criticism should be allowed while brainstorming. All ideas should be written down, no matter how crazy they seem. Remember, some of the best ideas seem very crazy at first glance.

4. Students should not only contribute original ideas, but they should also build upon the ideas already presented. Some call this "piggy-backing."

5. Props like a grab bag of items can be used to stimulate creativity.

6. After the session is over, have students select the top three ideas and write about why they like these ideas the most.

After a brainstorming session, students should judge the ideas using some sort of criteria. These criteria can include questions like: *Will it work? Is it too complicated to implement? Will others accept it? Is it a temporary or permanent solution? Is it cost effective?*

Using criteria to evaluate the brainstorming results is helpful for many reasons. It helps to solve a problem in a reasonable way by which the class can agree upon the solution. Students will see that evaluating the results is a necessary part of the creative process. Evaluation helps students to consider many perspectives of a problem. It is also good for students to explore the values related to the problem. Finally, the evaluation process proves that some of the most far-fetched ideas are the best solutions to a problem.

For example, suppose a school has a very high tardy rate. A teacher might present the following question a day ahead of time to the class for brainstorming: *How can we get more students to arrive at school on time?* Before the brainstorming session, the teacher should remind students that there will be no criticism during the brainstorming session, one person will speak at a time, and all ideas will be considered. One by one, students' ideas should be recorded on the board. After five minutes, the teacher stops the group and they evaluate the ideas using set criteria.

Brainstorming can take on many variations. One variation is *stop-and-go brainstorming*. After five minutes of gathering ideas, the teacher can stop the group and then have the group briefly evaluate the ideas and then continue brainstorming with another evaluation after five minutes.

Another variation is called *reverse brainstorming*. The problem is turned around and students brainstorm for ideas to help them see new viewpoints. For example: *How can costs be increased? How can we stimulate tardiness?* With reverse brainstorming, students are actually listing the causes of the problem.

Brainwriting is a variation that helps students to hitchhike ideas from each other. Students should work in small groups. One student writes down a solution to the problem, then the paper is passed to another student who writes a completely new idea on the paper, modifies the original idea, or uses the original idea to stimulate another related idea. The process continues until the paper gets back to the original writer. Then the group evaluates the ideas on the paper.

Some teachers who have a technology-savvy group might want to try *electronic brainstorming*. These types of brainstorming sessions can be accomplished through electronic messaging, discussion boards, chat rooms, or e-mail. This way no one has to wait in order to give an idea. With no face-to-face interaction, some students might be able to overcome their anxiety of criticism as well.

More Brainstorming Methods

Brainstorming not only can be used for creative problem solving, but it can also be used to generate a list of new ideas. This technique is called the *Attribute Listing Method.*

Robert Crawford, the designer of the Attribute Listing Method, believed that every time we take a creative step, we do it by changing the attributes of something. These attributes can then be modified (1954).

For example, if students want to create a new type of chips, they would first identify important attributes of chips with which they are already familiar. A chart can be made on the board with the following headings: *flavors, shapes, colors,* and *sizes.* Under each heading, students can list the qualities of chips. For example, under colors, students may list *orange, white, yellow, blue,* and *black.* Then, students think of ways to improve each attribute or good combinations can be chosen from the list.

If a toy store has an overabundance of scooters in its warehouse, students can be asked to change one or more parts of the scooters to make them really different in hopes of selling them. Students would list the parts of a scooter. Then under each part, changes would be listed in a chart format.

Suppose your school has bought all new desks. How can the old desks be put to use? First, have students list the qualities of a desk in a chart. Then, have them list the qualities or changes that they could make to the desks so that they can be used in another way around the school.

An extension of the Attribute Listing Method is *Morphological Synthesis.* A matrix grid is drawn with one attribute listed along the left hand side and another set of attributes listed along the top of the matrix. The two attributes or ideas combine in the cells of the matrix to create a new attribute or idea. Suppose students want to invent a new flavor of ice cream. Students can use the matrix grid on page 18 to create 100 new flavors of ice cream. A blank matrix grid is also provided on page 25.

Matrix Grid to Create New Flavors of Ice Cream

	vanilla	cake batter	bubble gum	berry	coconut	pineapple	coffee	cheesecake	rocky road	white chocolate
cherry										
strawberry										
peach										
lemon sherbet										
orange sherbet										
peppermint										
lime										
peanut butter										
cookie										
chocolate										

Brainstorming can be formatted into an idea checklist to help generate new products. One idea checklist is called SCAMPER (Osborn, 1953). Each letter stands for a way to change the product or item.

S	Substitute—components, materials, people
C	Combine—mix, combine with other assemblies or services, integrate
A	Adapt—alter, change function, use part of another element
M	Modify, Minify, or Magnify—increase or reduce in scale, change shape, attributes
P	Put to another use
E	Elaborate or Eliminate—remove elements, simplify, reduce to core functionality
R	Reverse or Rearrange

Sample SCAMPER activity: First, read the passage below.

> The Ring Lady was a famous skeleton found by archaeologists in a boat-house in nearby Herculaneum, Italy (also destroyed and buried by Mt. Vesuvius in A.D. 79). Along with her skeleton were found two gold rings, two gold bracelets, and two earrings for pierced ears. Archaeologists have deducted that these articles were jewelry used by the woman. Thieves stole these jewelry items in 1990. Luckily, archaeologists had made pictures of her jewels.

Find a picture of the Ring Lady; then complete the following SCAMPER activity using the blank SCAMPER chart on page 24.

Substitute: If the Ring Lady did not have pierced ears, in what other way could she have used the earrings that archaeologists think were made for pierced ears?

Combine: Jewelry gives messages based on how it is made and what pictures it displays. On her ring was a strutting bird and on her bracelets were two snakes. If you could combine these images onto one piece of jewelry, along with anything else, what message would that piece of jewelry send?

Adapt: Imagine that the Ring Lady was allergic to gold. What could have been her purpose for having these gold jewelry items with her at the time of her death?

Modify/Minify/Magnify: Archaeologists believe that the Ring Lady was "homely," but her elaborate jewelry shows that she was well cared for. What kind of feelings does this stir up in you toward the Ring Lady? How would your feelings change if she was described as a beautiful rich princess, or an ugly wretched witch, or a mean old stepmother?

Put to another use: Jewelry isn't only used for adorning oneself. What are some other ways that the Ring Lady's jewelry could have been used in everyday life?

Elaborate/Eliminate: The gold jewelry items were the only things by the skeleton that lasted for two thousand years, before the Ring Lady was discovered by archaeologists. What other items could have survived two thousand years with her body if she had chosen to be buried with them?

Reverse/Rearrange: Skeletons tell us many things about a person. Scientists know that she was female, 45 years old, and what she possibly looked like almost two thousand years ago. What if the Ring Lady had turned out to be a slave? What would the general public think about her?

Ideas for Classroom Brainstorming

1. **Brainstorming:** Suppose you just bought a pizza restaurant and want to expand your business to other countries. Your recent research reveals that people in other countries don't just like traditional toppings, such as cheese, pepperoni, and sausage. They want toppings of food found in their own culture. What kinds of toppings would someone who lives in Mexico like? What kinds of toppings would people who live in China like? How about in Saudi Arabia? Give each pizza a name and list its ingredients.

2. **Reverse Brainstorming:** There is a theft problem in your school. Try reverse brainstorming. What types of things can be done to make the theft problem worse in your school? Do any of these ideas give you some ways for making the school a theft-free place?

3. **Attribute Listing:** You are a writer/producer working for one of the major TV networks. They need a new idea for a show that would air on Saturday mornings. Make four columns. In the first column, list all the interesting characters you can think of. In the second column, list some ideas for plots (saving the planet, feeding the homeless, caring for pets) for the story line. In the third column, list problems that the characters might have, such as: they can't walk, they have no home, they have no power, or they are angry. In the fourth column, list some solutions that the characters find in the story, such as finding courage in unknown people, discovering hope in a hopeless situation, or persuading others to change their minds. Finally, choose three characters from the first column and one or two ideas from the second, third, and fourth columns. Use these ideas to write a sketch for your Saturday morning show.

4. **SCAMPER** can be used with people or things from history. Try this activity with the Revolutionary figure of Abigail Adams:

   Substitute: If Abigail Adams lived today, how would she communicate with her husband John Adams?

   Combine: In your opinion, what other events in Abigail Adams' life would be interesting to know about?

   Adapt: If Abigail Adams lived today, what modern figure would she resemble?

   Modif/Minify/Magnify: What if Abigail Adams had not written any letters? How would we know about her life?

   Put to another use: What if John Adams had used his legal training to prosecute the Boston Massacre defendants instead of defending them? How would the trial outcome have been different?

   Elaborate/Eliminate: What if John Adams had not listened to his wife? How would her life have been different?

   Reverse/Rearrange: What if the British had won the Revolution? How would John and Abigail Adams' lives have changed?

5. **SCAMPER** can also be used with books. Try this activity with the storybooks about the epic of Gilgamesh. The books are titled: *Gilgamesh the King, The Revenge of Ishtar,* and *The Last Quest of Gilgamesh* by Ludmila Zeman.

   Substitute: The goddess, Ishtar, kills Gilgamesh's dear friend, Enkidu. Gilgamesh then sets out on a quest for eternal life. If you could change the reason that Gilgamesh sets out to overcome death, what would it be?

   Combine: If you could combine Ishtar, the goddess of love, and Humbaba, the monster who hid in the forest, what kind of character would you have? Describe and draw this new character.

Adapt: Gilgamesh learned that the good he could accomplish in his kingdom during his lifetime was his immortality. How can this lesson that Gilgamesh learned be applied to you and your life?

Modify/Minify/Magnify: What if Gilgamesh had attained immortality? How would the story have ended? Rewrite the ending of Gilgamesh, telling what he did with this immortality.

Put to another use: Utanapishtim offered Gilgamesh a plant that would keep him young, but not necessarily keep him from dying. If Gilgamesh had been able to keep this plant, how could he have used it in his kingdom for the good of his people instead of for selfish means? Write a persuasive letter to Gilgamesh urging him to follow your advice.

Elaborate/Eliminate: Gilgamesh's quest took him to the house of Siduri, who gave him directions to Utanapishtim, the only mortal to have attained eternal life. Eliminate the female tavern owner, Siduri, from the story. How else would Gilgamesh have found his way?

Reverse/Rearrange: Rearrange all three picture books in the opposite order in which they were intended. Could the story make sense if events were reversed? Create a flow chart with this rearranged story.

SCAMPER

S Substitute	C Combine	A Adapt	M Modify Magnify Minify	P Put to Other Uses	E Elaborate Eliminate	R Reverse Rearrange

Blank Matrix Grid

Chapter 1 Review

1. What are some general guidelines when brainstorming with a class?
   a. resist criticism
   b. set aside a specific time for brainstorming
   c. allow students to build upon ideas already presented
   d. All of the above
   e. only a and b

2. Why should we evaluate brainstorming using criteria?
   a. Students need to see that evaluation is a necessary part of the creative process.
   b. It is good for students to explore the values related to the problem.
   c. It helps students to consider many perspectives of a problem.
   d. Evaluation proves that some of the far-fetched ideas are sometimes the best solutions to a problem.
   e. All of the above

3. What are some ways to brainstorm?
   a. Morphological matrix
   b. SCAMPER
   c. Attribute Listing Method
   d. All of the above

4. True or False? All ideas should be judged immediately during a brainstorming session.

Chapter 2 Pre-Reading Reflection

1. What is a graphic organizer?

   _____

   _____

   _____

   _____

2. Why do graphic organizers help students retain information?

   _____

   _____

   _____

   _____

3. Why is a graphic organizer sometimes referred to as a "map"?

   _____

   _____

   _____

   _____

Graphic Organizers

When working with very young children, what is the best way to have them classify different kinds of animals? How about getting them to explain the connections between certain characters in a story? Is it possible to get elementary-age children to remember the specific parts of a story? How can they best explain the rock cycle to their classmates? In what ways can middle and high school students show the key reasons for the Civil War? Will they ever be able to differentiate between the different instruments in a band?

There are answers to all these (and many more) questions. The answers lie in the use of graphic organizers. Graphic organizers help students stay focused on the task at hand. They visually demonstrate how information and ideas are organized. They also show us how students think. The graphic organizer is a picture worth a thousand words.

What Are Graphic Organizers?

Graphic organizers are visual representations of information that help us gather and sort pertinent information. They allow the mind to see patterns and relationships between information. More often than not, these organizers are called "maps" because they help us map out our ideas in a visual way.

Perhaps the most common graphic organizer that people see on a daily basis is the calendar. Calendars help us sort, sift, record, and share information. In recent years, graphic organizers have taken on the following names, just to name a few—semantic maps, webs, concept maps, story maps, and semantic organizers.

Graphic organizers have a way of connecting several pieces of isolated information. They take new information and file it into an existing framework. Old information is retrieved in the process and the new information is attached.

Pages 31 and 32 show several examples of filled-in graphic organizers to show how they can be used in the classroom for a variety of topics. Blank graphic organizers are provided later in the chapter for your classroom use.

Flow Charts and Time Lines

These graphic organizers help students to show sequence in a process or a series of events. The same basic process is required—placing one thing or idea after another according to the order in which they occurred.

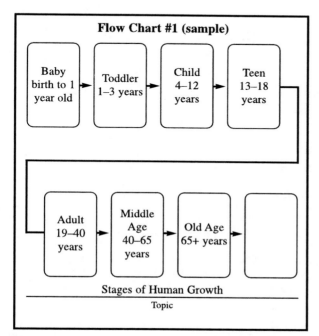

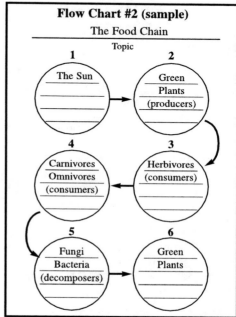

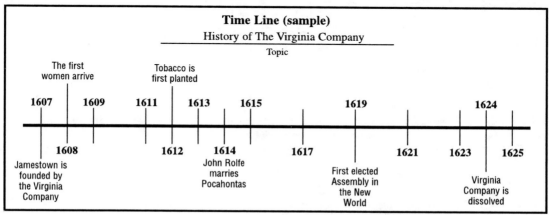

Excerpted from *Successful Strategies for Reading in the Content Areas: Grades 3–5.* Copyright © 2004 by Shell Education.

Concept Wheel

The main idea of the entire passage goes in the center circle and the details from the whole passage that answer the questions radiate from the main idea like spokes on a wheel.

Venn Diagram

To use the Venn diagram, students list unique characteristics of two ideas, things, or events (one in the outside section of the left circle and one in the outside section of the right circle). In the middle section where the circles overlap, students list characteristics that the two have in common.

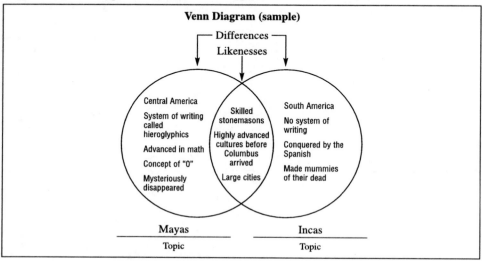

Excerpted from *Successful Strategies for Reading in the Content Areas: Grades 3–5*. Copyright © 2004 by Shell Education.

Why Use Graphic Organizers?

Understanding how the brain works helps us understand why graphic organizers are valuable tools for learning. In the book *Science Continuum of Concepts for Grades K–6*, Karen Olsen states:

> From brain research we have come to understand that the brain is a pattern-seeking device in search of meaning and that learning is the acquisition of mental programs for using what we understand. Thus, the most usable and useful curriculum for classroom teachers would be one that made clear for teacher and student what the patterns are and how those understandings would be used in the real world. (Olsen, 1995, p. 5)

Other researchers say that graphic organizers are one of the most powerful ways to build semantic memories (Sprenger, 1999). Eric Jensen says that semantic memory is "activated by association, similarities, or contrasts" and graphic organizers assist students with such necessary connections (1998, p. 106).

How does the brain do this? The brain stores information much like the way that a graphic organizer shows information. It screens large amounts of information and looks for patterns that are linked together. The brain is able to take meaning much easier from a visual format like a graphic organizer than from merely written words on a page. Graphic organizers not only help students manage information, but they offer information that students can understand at a glance. When connections are made on paper, the information engages other parts of the brain. When these connections happen, the brain transfers the information from short-term memory to long-term memory.

Using graphic organizers enriches students' reading abilities. First of all, graphic organizers help students learn to focus on key concepts taken from a text or broad idea.

As a result, they help students understand how concepts develop and evolve. As already mentioned, graphic organizers take new knowledge and integrate it with prior knowledge.

Using graphic organizers also enriches students' writing abilities. When students fill out graphic organizers, they learn to summarize information. Students cannot merely copy information to their page. When using graphic organizers, students have to think about how to write the information in a different way. This provides a unique way for students to take notes during a lecture or while reading a passage. Graphic organizers are also a great way to assess and evaluate students' learning.

Finally, using graphic organizers enriches students' thinking abilities. Especially when used with the brainstorming technique, graphic organizers can help students generate creative ideas. These organizers also help students clarify their thinking and demonstrate their understanding of a topic.

It is important to consider learning styles. Many students are visual learners. Visual learners remember information better through pictures, like graphic organizers. Students get into the habit of thinking in terms of symbols or key words. Not only are graphic organizers a great tool for those who are already visual thinkers, they are a great tool for helping others become stronger visual thinkers.

Ideas for Using Graphic Organizers

Graphic organizers can be used before, during, and after instruction in a classroom. They help us predict, plan, organize and reorganize, interpret, and compare and contrast.

Graphic organizers can be used for:

- Brainstorming
- Note-taking while reading a text or listening to a lecture
- Summarizing and organizing information
- Prewriting tools
- Comparing and contrasting information
- Finding the main idea and supporting details
- Showing sequence of events
- Organizing a story
- Finding cause and effect relationships
- Character maps/traits
- Differentiating between facts and opinions
- Helping with decision making
- Showing cycles
- Finding the 5 Ws

Look at the following pages for printed samples of graphic organizers that you can copy and use in your classroom.

The maps below can be used to record the main idea and supporting details of any passage or book.

Star Map

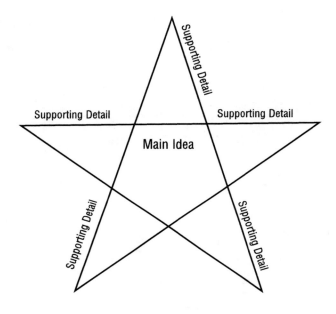

Spider Map

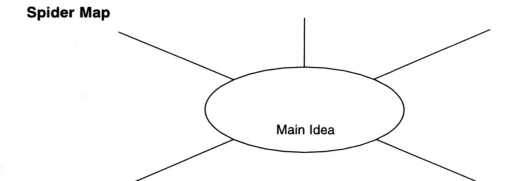

Compare-and-Contrast Matrix

The chart below can be used to record information about two groups of people, places, or things that are being compared and contrasted.

Attribute	Item 1	Item 2
Attribute 1		
Attribute 2		
Attribute 3		

Fishbone Map

The map below can be used to organize information that describes how an event occurred.

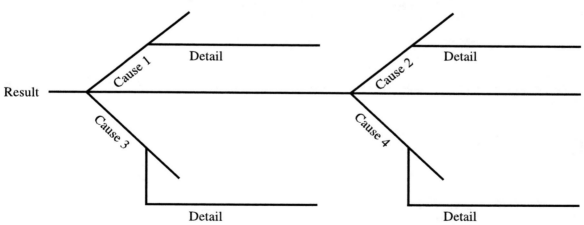

Note-taking Wheel

The following graphic organizer can be used to take notes on significant information. When taking notes, remember to:

- ❏ Use short phrases, not complete sentences.
- ❏ Use your own words.
- ❏ Write quickly, don't worry about handwriting, spelling, or grammar.
- ❏ Use abbreviations when possible.

⇧ **Important People**

⇧ **Setting – Time and Place**

Events

Other Important Facts

⇩

⇩

Excerpted from *Successful Strategies for Reading in the Content Areas: Grades 3–5*. Copyright © 2004 by Shell Education.

Semantic Map

The following semantic map can be used to take notes about the key concept in the center, about the subtopics in the outer circles, and about the details on the lines.

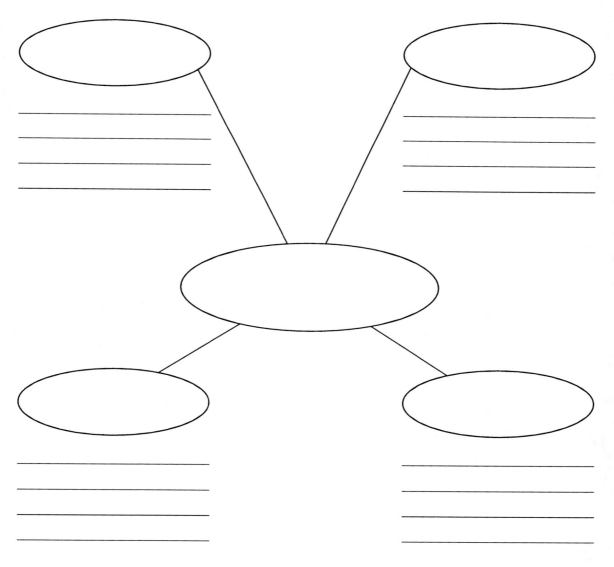

Decision Tree

This chart can be used to outline a problem, three possible solutions, and the advantages and disadvantages of each solution.

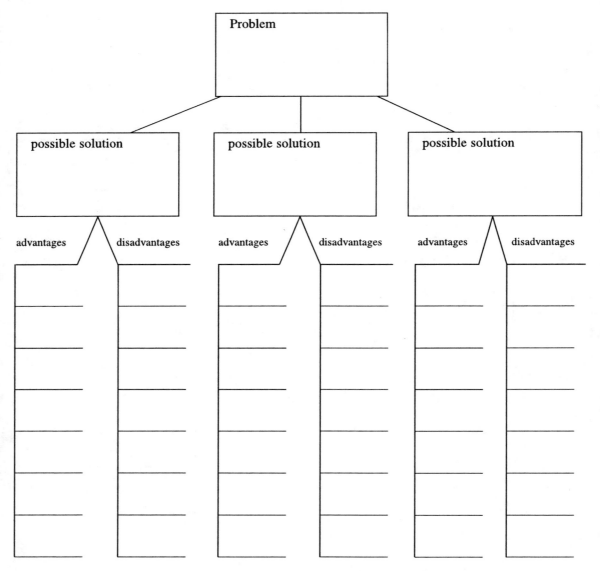

Excerpted from *Successful Strategies for Reading in the Content Areas: Grades 3–5*. Copyright © 2004 by Shell Education.

Text Graph

The following chart can be used to illustrate the events in any text. Events that are positive are to be illustrated in the top half of the chart and events that are negative are to be illustrated in the bottom half of the chart. Use the +5 to –5 rating system to indicate the degree of positive or negative associated with the event. The center horizontal line is "0."

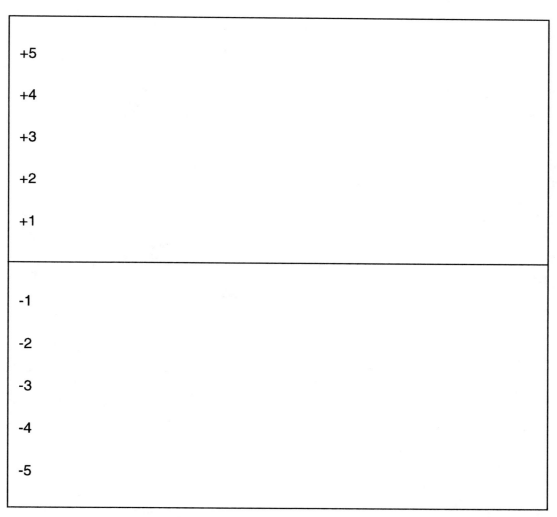

Storyboard Planner

The following planner can be used to illustrate the events, process, or steps as they occur in any text.

Event #1	Event #2	Event #3
Event #4	Event #5	Event #6
Event #7	Event #8	Event #9
Event #10	Event #11	Event #12

Excerpted from *Successful Strategies for Reading in the Content Areas: Grades 3–5*. Copyright © 2004 by Shell Education.

Chapter 2 Review

1. Why should we use graphic organizers?
    a. The brain stores information much like the way that a graphic organizer shows information. It screens large amounts of information and looks for patterns that are linked together.
    b. Graphic organizers offer information that students can understand at a glance.
    c. Graphic organizers help students manage information.
    d. All of the above

2. Graphic organizers are called "maps" because . . .
    a. they help us find our destination.
    b. they help us map out our ideas in a visual way.
    c. they are tools for learning much like a map is a tool for a traveler.

3. Graphic organizers enrich a student's reading ability by _____.
    a. clarifying his/her thinking and demonstrating his/her understanding of a topic
    b. focusing on key concepts taken from a text or a broad idea
    c. explaining how to write the new information in a different way

4. When should graphic organizers be used?
    a. before instruction
    b. during instruction
    c. after instruction
    d. All of the above

Chapter 3 Pre-Reading Reflection

1. What makes a question a *good* question?

   _____

   _____

   _____

   _____

   _____

2. What types of questions should teachers ask students?

   _____

   _____

   _____

   _____

   _____

3. Why is it important to model good questioning techniques to students?

   _____

   _____

   _____

   _____

   _____

Questioning
Techniques

In any given classroom today, a teacher will ask about 80 questions every hour. In that same classroom, only two questions per hour will come from the students. What does this say about our classrooms today? First of all, it says that teachers are spending a lot of time asking questions. But experience tells us that these questions are mostly "yes" and "no" questions and strictly recall questions. It also tells us that teachers, not students, are doing the asking. That means today's students are mostly passive learners, not active ones.

What would a classroom be like where students were asking most of the questions? It is important to note that students will only know how to ask the questions that are modeled by the teacher. So, what kinds of questions should those be? The answer is both simple and complex—they should be *good* questions.

What makes a question a good question? Think about this question for a minute. Do you want to know the answer? Does it make you pause and think? Does this question strike you as a broad one with many answers? Could this be a good question in itself? The right kinds of questions make students think. Many of these good questions are developed from curiosity. Good questions may have many right answers or no right answers at all. They stem from a desire to acquire information. Even Socrates and Plato urged their students to question incessantly. Good questions make learning meaningful.

Why Is Questioning so Important?

Questions are the tools that bring insight and understanding. They bring sense to a confusing world. Some say questioning is the most powerful tool ever created.

Can we think without questions? What does the word *think* mean anyway? Webster's Dictionary defines *think* as "to form ideas, conceive, judge, consider, or arrive at conclusions." According to this definition, regurgitating is not thinking. To think is to be actively engaged in learning. To have great thinkers, we must have great questions. But not all forms of thinking are the same. Thinking occurs at various degrees depending on the depth of the questions.

Questioning is important for many reasons. First of all, questioning has so much to do with communicating with one another. Many of our conversations revolve around questions. In other words, without questions, we would not have many conversations. Questioning also helps us avoid mistakes. It improves our study skills by making us independent learners. Questioning expands our knowledge and thinking ability. It gets us wondering and pondering the unknown. But most importantly, by using the right questioning techniques, teachers serve as a model by teaching students the right kinds of questions to ask. Teaching students how to question will transform our students from being passive learners to active learners. They will become problem solvers who can make decisions.

What Questions Should We Ask?

A good question can begin with any of these words—
Why, How, and *Which*. When a question begins with
why, students analyze cause-and-effect relationships.
Most questions asked by young children begin with the
word *why*. It is the word used for figuring out answers.
*Why does the sun come up each day? Why does the roos-
ter crow at dawn? Why do plants die?*

Questions that begin with *how* tend to be problem-solving questions. It is a level of synthesis. These types of
questions seek to change and improve things. Inventors
ask the *how* questions. It is the *how* questions that spurn
new inventions, improve businesses, and repair items.
*How will the prince win her love? How will the hero
emerge from the war? How can I get my computer to
work faster?*

Finally, questions that begin with *which* are decision-
making questions. These questions require thoughtful
choices based on evidence or clearly-stated criteria.
Which questions are the most important questions of all
because they often determine who we will become.
*Which city is best to live in? Which road will I travel in
life? Which plan is the best?*

A teacher should model these questions, and, most
importantly, students should be asking them, too. In the
past few years, studies show that students have not been
the ones asking the questions. Instead, teachers have
fired off recall questions every three seconds or so.

There are numerous models of questioning. In this chapter we will explore Bloom's Taxonomy of the Cognitive
Domain, Williams' Taxonomy of Creative Thought, and
the Three Story Intellect Model.

Socratic Seminar as a Questioning Strategy

It is no coincidence that the term *Socratic Seminar* sounds like the name Socrates. Questioning was at the very core of what he taught his students in Athens. He firmly believed skepticism to be a positive trait. His classroom became famous and popular because of his rigorous questions. This attracted many notable students. Needless to say, his model of questioning is one that has stood the test of time.

The Socratic Seminar examines ideas, principles, and issues. Before conducting a seminar, students should be very familiar with the topic or issue at hand. The seminar can be about a primary source document, a painting, or an issue being debated on the local news.

The role of the teacher is to prepare the open-ended questions that explore ideas, values, and issues. These are not questions that focus on facts already known. These questions should encourage participation, and the teacher should encourage students to address one another during the discussion if a conflict or disagreement arises.

The teacher is also the one asking the questions. These questions should be open-ended and should focus upon ideas and themes related to the topic. In addition, the questions should capture students' interests.

Sample questions include:

- What would you cite to defend the actions of . . . ?
- What information would you use to support the view . . . ?
- How would you justify . . . ?
- Why was it better that . . . ?
- How would you compare ideas . . . ?

Using the sample questions on page 48 or any others of your choice, do the following example of a Socratic Seminar with your students.

On the day of the seminar, have students sit in a large circle, with yourself as part of that circle. Lead the discussion by asking a question. When students answer, other students may speak their mind too, but only one person should speak at a time. When there is no more discussion on that question, move on to another question that has been prepared beforehand, repeating the same process. The goal is to get students to think critically and to model how to ask questions.

Closing questions should help students see the big picture. Students can point out the most important aspect of a piece. Students can also reflect on how their opinions have changed since the discussion.

Sample closing questions include:

- What would you select as the most important aspect of this piece?
- What caused you to change your mind during the discussion?
- What have you learned about this piece?
- How will your new knowledge enable you to be a better person?

If the discussion has historical value, have students talk about the actual historic event. Students can also reflect on the discussion in a journal or writing activity for homework.

Bloom's Taxonomy

In 1956, educator Benjamin Bloom worked with a group of educational psychologists to classify levels of cognitive thinking. Bloom's Taxonomy has been used in class-rooms over the last 40 years as a hierarchy of questions that progresses from less difficult to more complex. The progression allows teachers to identify the level at which students are thinking. It also provides a framework for introducing a variety of questions to students as well as differentiating according to students' ability levels.

Many teachers see this taxonomy as a ladder or pyramid. For example, some teachers think they have to begin at the bottom with knowledge questions and work their way progressively up to the evaluative questions. But that is not necessary to achieve good questions for students. For example, a question can begin with analysis. Students can be challenged to figure out why test scores are low in a particular district. This type of question requires students to acquire, analyze, and synthesize information to arrive at a solution. There are appropriate times for each level of questions.

Bloom's Taxonomy is a useful model for categorizing test questions. According to Bloom, as students move toward more advanced levels of thinking, they analyze by breaking things into smaller parts, synthesize when they think creatively, and evaluate when they make judgments based on evidence.

On the following pages, each level of Bloom's Taxonomy has four categories of information:

1. A description of the type of thinking that is involved.

2. Key verbs for teachers to use in asking a question at that level.

3. Typical products and activities that result from this level of thinking.

4. Specific question/sentence example prompts that represent Bloom's taxonomy.

Knowledge Skills

This cognitive skill requires that students:

- Recall or locate information
- Remember something previously learned
- Memorize information

When asking questions that require knowledge, the following verbs are used:

tell	recite	list
memorize	remember	define
locate	describe	identify
name	match	arrange
duplicate	label	order
recognize	relate	recall
repeat	reproduce	state

Products/activities resulting:

workbook pages	quizzes	tests
exams	vocabulary	facts in isolation

Specific examples of knowledge in the classroom:

Write the definitions of the following words.

Label the planets in the solar system.

Comprehension Skills

This cognitive skill requires that students:

- Understand and explain facts
- Demonstrate basic understanding of concepts and curriculum
- Translate to other words
- Grasp the meaning
- Interpret information
- Explain what happened in their own words (or pictures)

When asking questions that require comprehension, the following verbs are used:

restate	give examples	explain
summarize	translate	show symbols
edit	distinguish	estimate
predict	generalize	classify
describe	discuss	illustrate
express	identify	indicate
locate	recognize	report
restate	review	select

Products/activities resulting:

drawings	diagrams
response to questions	revisions

Specific examples of comprehension in the classroom:

What are some reasons why clouds bring rain?

Summarize the first chapter of the story.

Application Skills

This cognitive skill requires that students:

- Use prior learning to solve a problem or to answer a question
- Transfer knowledge learned in one situation to another
- Use new material in new and concrete situations
- Apply the lessons of the past to a situation today

When asking questions that require application, the following verbs are used:

demonstrate	build	cook
compute	prepare	solve
produce	discover	choose
apply	dramatize	employ
illustrate	operate	practice
schedule	sketch	chart
use	write	

Products/activities resulting:

recipes	models	artwork
demonstrations	crafts	

Specific examples of application in the classroom:

Take the specific data and put it into a bar graph.

Consider how you feel about the dress code and draw a picture that represents your feelings.

Analysis Skills

This cognitive skill requires that students:

- See in-depth relationships between and among parts of the information
- Understand how parts relate to a whole
- Understand structure and motive
- Note fallacies
- Break down material into its component parts so that its organizational structure can be understood
- Take a complicated situation and break it down into its parts

When asking questions that require analysis, the following verbs are used:

investigate	classify	examine
categorize	compare	contrast
solve	diagram	differentiate
illustrate	outline	distinguish
separate		

Products/activities resulting:

Venn diagrams	lists of attributes	surveys
solutions	conclusions	

Specific examples of analysis in the classroom:

Compare and contrast the current president's campaign promises to those of President Abraham Lincoln.

In what ways could a large influx of migrants change a community?

Synthesis Skills

This cognitive skill requires that students:

- Create new ideas by pulling parts of the information together
- Reform individual parts to make a new whole
- Take a jumble of facts and add them up to make sense

When asking questions that require synthesis, the following verbs are used:

compose	design	invent
create	hypothesize	construct
forecast	imagine	categorize
combine	compile	reconstruct
summarize	plan	write
arrange	assemble	collect
develop	formulate	manage
organize	prepare	propose
rearrange parts	set up	

Products/activities resulting:

original plans	hypothesis	creative stories
compositions	inventions	experiments

Specific examples of synthesis in the classroom:

Create a new song about the continents that goes to the melody of "Twinkle, Twinkle, Little Star."

Write a new ending to the book *Hatchet* or any other classic book.

Evaluation Skills

This cognitive skill requires that students:

- Make judgments based on evidence
- Determine the value of something, i.e., criteria
- Support judgment
- Consider the value of material for a given purpose
- Examine a person/policy/event and tell whether it measures up to a certain standard

When asking questions that require evaluation, the following verbs are used:

judge	evaluate	give opinions
viewpoint	prioritize	recommend
critique	appraise	compare
conclude	justify	criticize
interpret	argue	assess
defend	estimate	predict
rate	support	value

Products/activities resulting:

rating ideas	making judgments	book reviews
editorials	self assessments	

Specific examples of evaluation in the classroom:

Justify the decision made by the principal to require uniforms for students at school.

Decide whether you agree or disagree with the statement "Lying is always bad." Be prepared to support your decision.

Williams' Taxonomy of Creative Thought

Williams' Taxonomy of Creative Thought has eight levels of questions that expand a student's creativity. All eight of these questions are an extension of Bloom's synthesis levels of thinking. The first four levels are of the cognitive domain, while the last four levels of questions work with the affective domain.

1. **Fluency**—Questions generate a great many ideas, related answers, or choices.

2. **Flexibility**—Questions encourage flexibility and seek to change everyday objects so that an array of categories is generated. Detours are taken and sizes, shapes, quantities, time limits, requirements, objectives, or dimensions are varied.

3. **Elaboration**—Questions expand, enlarge, enrich, or embellish possibilities that build on prior ideas or thoughts.

4. **Originality**—Questions promote originality and seek new ideas by suggesting unusual twists to change content or to generate clever responses.

5. **Curiosity**—Questions promote curiosity and allow students to follow a hunch, question alternatives, ponder outcomes, and wonder about options.

6. **Risk taking**—Questions deal with the unknown by asking students to take chances, try new things, or experiment with new ideas.

7. **Complexity**—Questions create structure in an unstructured setting. They can also build a logical order in a given situation.

8. **Imagination**—Questions encourage imagination and help students visualize possibilities, build images in the mind, picture new objects, and reach beyond the practical limits.

The Odyssey and Williams' Taxonomy

Using the passage below and students' knowledge of *The Odyssey*, practice the eight levels of questions of Williams' Taxonomy of Creative Thought with your students.

Odysseus, king of Ithaca, has made his way homeward and has reclaimed his rightful place. You feared that he (and you) might not make it, seeing that his quest for home took 17 years from the time he left Ithaca. This long trip has made you tired, but you are also eager to tell your story in a new light.

Have students expand their creative knowledge of *The Odyssey* with the exercises below.

Fluency

You are an Oscar-winning screenwriter and have been commissioned to write a screenplay for *The Odyssey*. While writing this screenplay, you have envisioned several actors for the main roles. If anyone could be cast for the main roles, who would they be? The main roles include Odysseus, Penelope, Telemachus, crew of five comrades, three evil suitors, and Athena.

Flexibility

Pick a time in history in which this epic tale would be set. Remember, the time in history will have bearing on the costumes, problems/conflicts that arise, and transportation Odysseus takes to get home to "Ithaca." Explain how the setting affects each of these—costumes, problems and conflicts, and transportation.

Elaboration

Elaborate on the scene where Odysseus and his crew are trapped in the cave with the Cyclops. Tell the story from the Cyclops's point of view. Remember, he is Poseidon's son.

Originality

Decide on a new name for Odysseus, king of Ithaca. Choose a name with substantial meaning for this quest. Search through baby name books and the Internet to gain ideas.

Curiosity

Odysseus and his men safely passed the first peril of the Sirens about which Circe had warned them. What do you think would have happened to Odysseus and his men if they had landed on the island with the Sirens? Create a brief script in the form of a dream to show what would have taken place on that island with the Sirens.

Risk Taking

You are afraid that the name *The Odyssey* would not bring many viewers to this potential box office hit. Create a poster and rename this screenplay to make it more electrifying to the general public.

Complexity

How would the movie fare if the gods had not intervened? Choose a part of the book where the gods helped Odysseus and decide on another way Odysseus could have combated the problem. (Remember, Athena and Hermes both interceded help when needed.)

Imagination

Close your eyes and imagine how this movie would fare if the following movie stars played Odysseus—Arnold Schwarzenegger, Jackie Chan, Eddie Murphy, or Homer Simpson. With each name, write the mood that each star would cast upon the setting.

The Three Story Intellect Model

> There are one-story intellects, two-story intellects, and three-story intellects with skylights. All fact collectors who have no aim beyond their facts are one-story people. Two-story people compare, reason, and generalize, using the labor of fact collectors as their own. Three-story people idealize, imagine, predict—their best illumination comes from above through the skylight. —Oliver Wendell Holmes (poet)

The Three Story Intellect Model (illustrated in Figure 3.1) is much like Bloom's Taxonomy, except that it categorizes thinking into three levels instead of six. The three levels work together in order to process information much like the brain works.

Level I, called the **Gathering** or **Input Phase**, describes how students gather information through their senses. This is the foundation for higher-level thinking. Students learn to state problems in their own words, observe and gather information for making decisions, create goals, and connect information with previous experiences. Level II is the **Processing Phase**. Information is processed to make it meaningful. Students build on the foundation of skills in Level I by comparing, inferring, organizing, and questioning information. In Level III, the **Applying Phase**, students incorporate all the levels of thinking. They generate new ideas by predicting, judging, imagining, and evaluating.

It is not necessary to advance in our thinking in a particular order. Thinking can begin at Level III with a problem for the students to solve. A problematic situation is one of the best ways to get students excited about learning. When students are confronted with a problem (Level III), they have to then gather information (Level I), process it (Level II) and then return to Level III to make a final decision.

Figure 3.1: Three Story Intellect Model

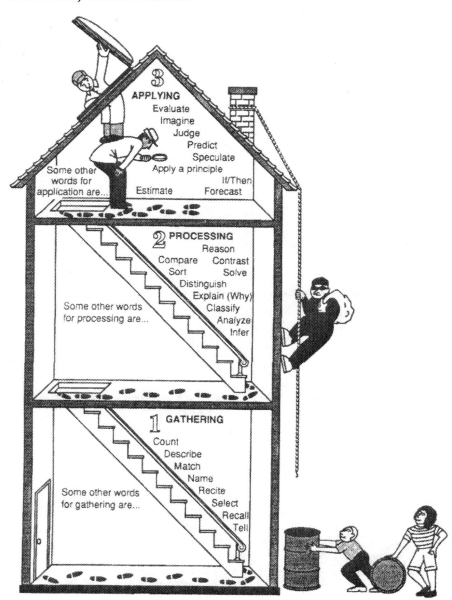

From *The Best of Skylight: Essential Teaching Tools* by James Bellanca. Reproduced by permission from LessonLab, a Pearson Education Company. Copyright © 2002 by Skylight Professional Development.

Sample Questions from the
Three Story Intellect Method:

Level I: Gathering Questions

How did the pioneers make their way out west?

Who is Bill Gates?

What did Napoleon accomplish for the people of France?

Why was the Declaration of Independence signed in Philadelphia?

Where is the island of Cyprus?

Level II: Processing Questions

How can you explain why terrorism occurs?

If you were a southern soldier in the Civil War, how would you feel about the battle at Gettysburg?

Why did the Boston Tea Party take place?

Compare the two main events in the story.

How do you know that the earth is always changing?

Level III: Application Questions

What kind of advice would Shakespeare give the president today?

How could you solve the problem of pollution in your town?

What would the world be like without death?

Which is the best dessert?

How would you justify war?

Chapter 3 Review

1. The following task would be an example of which one of the following stages of Bloom's Taxonomy? "Based on your understanding of the water cycle, illustrate the four main stages."
    a. Synthesis
    b. Application
    c. Analysis
    d. Evaluation
    e. Comprehension

2. Which stage of Bloom's Taxonomy requires students to recall specific facts?
    a. Knowledge
    b. Synthesis
    c. Application
    d. Analysis
    e. Evaluation

3. The following task would be an example of which one of the eight stages of Williams' Taxonomy? "How many questions can you write for the solution ten?"
    a. Flexibility
    b. Originality
    c. Complexity
    d. Fluency

4. The following task would be an example of which stage of the Three Story Intellect Model? "Take and defend a position on a U.S. citizen's right to own handguns."
    a. Gather
    b. Process
    c. Apply

Chapter 4 Pre-Reading Reflection

1. Why should we seek to engage students in identifying and solving problems?

   _____

   _____

   _____

   _____

   _____

2. What is the relationship between problem solving and learning?

   _____

   _____

   _____

   _____

   _____

3. What are the benefits of problem-based learning?

   _____

   _____

   _____

   _____

Problem-Based Learning

Imagine you are a student again. You are well aware that vandalism is on the rise in your school. Lockers have been broken into, students' belongings have been stolen, furniture has been scratched, and walls have been written on during school hours. The school has decided to implement safety measures. Hall passes will be strictly enforced, no outside recess will be permitted, and no one will be allowed to leave the cafeteria before their lunch time is over. These rules seem extreme to you. You feel that innocent students are being punished for what only a few do. There has to be a better way to stop the vandals. What can you do?

Your teacher allows you to work in groups to generate possible ideas or solutions to this problem. You decide to write a petition, form volunteer patrols, and survey students. You identify available information related to this problem, such as reviewing school policies, viewing a sample petition, and looking at parts of the school that have been vandalized. You identify issues that need to be investigated further, i.e., how to form patrols, what other schools are doing, and how to write a survey. Your group finds resources to consult. These might include policies from other schools, the police force, and sample surveys. Group members are assigned one of the tasks above and information is gathered and recorded. Finally, your group is ready to propose a solution and you present your solution to the school board. This type of learning is called *problem-based learning.*

What Is Problem-Based Learning?

Problem-based learning, as we know it today, was first used in the 1950s at Case Western Reserve University. It is currently used by more than 80% of medical schools to train students about medicine.

> Problem-based learning is a curriculum development and instructional system that simultaneously develops both problem-solving strategies and disciplinary knowledge bases and skills by placing students in the active role of problem solvers confronted with an ill-structured problem that mirrors real-world problems. (Finkle & Torp, 1995, p. 1)

Problem-based learning gives students the opportunity to collaborate with their classmates as they study the issues of a certain problem. They use the information they find to try and create viable solutions. Instead of listening to teacher-led lectures in a classroom, students participate in small-group discussions. The amount of direct instruction in a problem-based classroom is very limited, so students have to take on the responsibility for their own learning. The teacher's role is much like a coach—he/she presents the problematic situation, becomes the subject matter expert, resource guide, and consultant, as well as a co-investigator that keeps students on task. The teacher asks the questions like "Why? What do you mean? How do you know that is true?" He/she questions a student's logic and even hints at erroneous reasoning. He/she models critical thinking so that students will begin to ask each other the same kinds of questions. The student's role is a participant who grapples with the complexity of the situation while investigating and resolving the problem from the inside out.

Why Use Problem-Based Learning?

There are many reasons for using problem-based learning with students. First, we know that our minds are capable of thinking through complex situations. It is the nature of our survival on Earth. Research says that it is the complex challenges that develop our intellect and ability to think productively (Caine & Caine, 1997; Diamond & Hopson, 1998).

Problem-based learning also increases motivation in students. Students see that the outcome of their work can make a real difference in society. The main goal of problem-based learning is to engage students in learning. One cognitive theory states that students will work if presented with problems that are perceived as meaningful.

In addition, it provides the reason for learning information. It shows that what students do in school can have an impact in the real world. Even John Dewey said that school should be life-like instead of merely preparing students for life.

Problem-based learning promotes higher-level thinking skills. These types of problems do not provide just one right answer. Students are forced into thinking both critically and creatively as they seek to find solutions to problems. Perhaps the most important aspect of problem solving is analyzing problems versus simply performing a task or practicing a set of skills. Studies performed in other countries, such as Japan, show teachers beginning lessons with a challenge and asking students to analyze the many ways to solve the problem (Barell, 2003). Many of these countries have produced students who are well-trained to problem solve once they reach the workplace.

This type of learning provides opportunities for students to work with others in collaborative groups. In problem-based learning, students are required to listen to one another, synthesize information, and work as a group to solve problems. It prepares students for the workplace, where teamwork is both valued and required. Think about *Apollo 13*. The mission control staff on the ground in Houston had to work together to save the crew in outer space. Were it not for their teamwork, the crew of *Apollo 13* would not have survived.

Problem-based learning provides a learning atmosphere in which students can think about thinking, also called *metacognition*. Strategies are generated for defining a problem, gathering information, analyzing data, and building and testing a hypothesis. Problem identification without referring to a text book is a life skill (Barell, 2002b). Many state standardized tests call for inquiry. Inquiry is not limited to science alone. It is a skill that can and should be used in Language Arts and Social Studies, where students analyze conflicts in stories and in historical events.

Finally, authentic learning takes place in a classroom where problem-based learning is incorporated. A problem-solving context is the best way to acquire information (Tyler, 1949). The way that students are engaged in learning information is similar to the way in which students will recall it and use it in the future. Problem-based learning also assesses learning in ways that show student understanding.

How to Implement Problem-Based Learning

A typical problem-based learning lesson has several cycles. These steps can be repeated over and over as necessary to come to a conclusion.

Steps for Problem-Based Learning:

1. Locate the problem
2. Hook the students into the problem
3. Develop a problem statement—*How can we . . . in such a way that . . .*
4. Organize the problem with questions, research, and fact finding
5. Decide on an action plan
6. Create and present a final product
7. Assess

First, the teacher should locate a real-world problem. It is best if this problem can connect to learning standards and goals.

Next, the teacher determines facts and finds a way for students to enter the problem. Students tie it to something that they are interested in. This is called the *hook*.

After the problem has been presented, students discuss what they know to be the facts of the problem. Then students analyze the problem, brainstorm ideas about the problem, and create an exact statement of the problem. This is the *hypothesis*. The problem statement might sound like this:

How can we . . . in such a way that . . .

Next, students will need to identify information needed to understand the problem and identify resources to be used to gather information. Students will then find and share information by interviewing, collecting data, and performing other forms of research. They can revise the problem statement and ask additional questions if necessary. Remember, any of these steps can be repeated in the process as students grapple with the problem.

Next, students develop solutions by reasoning with information, finding a solution that fits best, as well as considering the consequences for their solution.

Lastly, students develop some sort of presentation where they explain, apply, and justify their solution to the problem. Their information can be published for others to see.

It is important to remember that the problem should not have a fixed or formulaic solution. There is not one right answer. The problem is generally described as messy and complex in nature. It requires questioning, information gathering, and reflection.

The chart on page 71 could be used in your classroom to help you and students organize the problem-solving process.

Directions: Use the chart to help organize the problem-solving process.

Problem	Idea/ Hunches	Facts	Questions	Action Plan

The KWHLAQ Strategy is another strategy that can be used to analyze a problem and organize information.

KWHLAQ Strategy

K	What do we think we **know** about the subject?
W	What do we **want** or need to know?
H	**How** will we go about finding answers to our questions?
L	What are we **learning** on a daily basis, and what have we **learned** after our culminating projects?
A	How can we **apply** the major concepts, ideas, principles, and skills to the same subject, to other subjects, and to our lives beyond the classroom?
Q	What new **questions** do we have now?

Examples of Problem-Based Learning

Ideas for problem-based learning can come from television, newspaper articles, or literature. Because students bring their own prior knowledge to develop ideas and then formulate those ideas into hypotheses, these scenarios can be used with almost any age group. The high school level will invariably produce a deeper investigation with complex results than will a younger classroom.

Possible scenarios:

1. You are a resident in a suburban area where the deer population has become problematic. Deer are eating up all the plants and the neighbors are complaining. It has even become dangerous to drive at night in the area for fear of hitting a deer. What action can be taken?

2. You are a widower who has a six-year-old son. When your wife died, you received $25,000 dollars in worker's compensation and $15,000 in stock option shares. You want your son to attend college after high school. How can you invest this money so that by that time, its growth is maximized?

3. You are a member of the President's staff of homeland security. Your particular area of expertise is the security of schools in the area. What advice will you give the President to help make schools more secure?

4. You are a member of the local school board. The book *Huckleberry Finn* has been included on a state censorship list. A session has been called to determine whether this book should be read in school classrooms or not. What arguments would you give for or against allowing this book to be read in classrooms?

5. The water in your town is not fit to drink. The grocery stores in town have seized upon this opportunity and are charging high prices for drinking water. What can you do about it?

6. The local museum in your town needs appropriate materials that explain organ function, effects of nutrition, and benefits of exercise for young children who visit the museum. The museum has contacted your class to provide these materials. How will you do it?

7. You are the superintendent of schools in your area. Student test scores are at an all time low in your district. Parents and school officials are worried. What can be done to raise these scores?

8. You are a local doctor in town. Recently, you have seen several mysterious cases of sickness that cannot be explained. The numbers are growing at an alarming rate. What can be done to stop the spread of the disease?

9. Your classroom has received a grant of $100 that will allow you to plant a vegetable garden. You must consider the weather in your area before you plant so that the vegetables will not die. What will you plant and what location will allow for the best crop?

10. Voter turnout has been pathetic in the past two local elections. You are a member of the local community group that advocates voter responsibility. How can you encourage people in your community to get out and vote?

Chapter 4 Review

1. True or False? Teachers use direct instruction during problem-based learning lessons.

2. True or False? Students can repeat the problem-solving steps several times over before coming to the conclusion to a problem.

3. Which of these are parts of the problem-solving process for problem-based learning?

   a. Develop a problem statement—*How can we . . . in such a way that . . .*

   b. Decide on an action plan

   c. Create and present a final product

   d. Organize the problem with questions, research, and fact finding

   e. All of the above

4. Problem-based learning is beneficial for students because _____.

   a. it provides opportunities for them to work together collaboratively.

   b. students need to see that there are problems in this world.

   c. if students don't start solving problems, they will never learn how.

Chapter 5 Pre-Reading Reflection

1. Try to think of an item or document that describes you.

   _____

   _____

2. What type of document is it?

   _____

3. How does the document relate to you?

   _____

   _____

4. What is the date of the document?

   _____

5. Who created the document?

   _____

6. What does this document say about the person who created it and the person who saved it?

   _____

   _____

7. What does this document tell us about life during that time period?

   _____

   _____

Primary Sources

Think about the school identity badges that so many teachers are required to wear today. What will this document tell people two hundred years from now? It will tell the person's name, show what that person looked like, and tell the date the badge was created. It will also tell the name of the school where this person worked. The fact that this document exists will tell that schools had to take security measures to keep children safe.

Think of a woman during the Great Depression who struggled to feed her family. Those facts become real when you see her written receipt showing that she traded chickens to pay for piano lessons for her child. What does that receipt tell us about how people had to live back then?

How about Michelangelo's statue of *David*, da Vinci's painting of the *Last Supper*, and Brunelleschi's architectural structure on the cathedral in Florence? All of these were created during the Renaissance in Italy. And all had a religious theme. What does that say about the time period and the role of the Church?

In ancient times, people used cylinder seals as their signature or personal stamp. These seals, made from small pieces of stone shaped like a tube, had special carvings on them. Ancient people would roll a cylinder seal on wet clay and it would leave an impression of an interesting design, picture, or written message. What do these impressions tell us about the ancient people who owned the seals?

Primary sources are a voice from the past and tell us more about life during the time period than even the best written book could tell. They provide an avenue by which we can touch history and make it personal. They offer us the opportunity to analyze and the opportunity to participate in history.

What Are Primary Sources?

Primary sources are a powerful learning and teaching device that provide students, teachers, and scholars with a window to the past unlike any other kind of resource. In some ways, just about everything around us can be deemed a primary source. A *primary source* is any documentation of an event from a person who actually participated in the event. Such sources give us a firsthand look at the past. Like the letters from someone's grandparents, these documents help the students define who they are and provide direction for the future.

Some examples of primary sources include:

- Columbus' Spotlight Journal from his first voyage to the New World

- A letter written by a general who survived the *USS Maine* explosion

- Recipes used during the Great Depression
- Comic books written during the Cold War
- Games played during Colonial Times
- *Lusitania* passenger log book
- Paintings from the Renaissance
- Photographs of Civil War generals
- Egyptian hieroglyphics
- Children's books used as Nazi propaganda during the Holocaust
- Revolutionary War cartoons printed by the English
- Maps from early explorers
- Sketches of Zheng He's ten masted ships
- Posters from WWII encouraging people to ration sugar

Why Use Primary Sources?

Using primary sources offers students the opportunity to act and think as historians. They participate in the constructive process of history by studying primary documents and photographs. History comes alive as students view historic photographs, handle facsimiles of famous documents, and read the comments and opinions of those in the past. When students understand the background of primary sources, they begin to put historical events and attitudes into perspective, think progressively, and walk in the shoes of their ancestors.

Primary sources don't have to be used only in history class. Introduce primary sources when reading works from particular authors. Primary sources can be used in math class when studying about different mathematicians. Artifacts from Galileo are particularly useful in science, too.

With an array of primary sources at your disposal, teachers can help connect students to the past in ways that are unimaginable. They enrich student understanding and give the past meaning. They enhance your repertoire of teaching tools by providing relevance and depth. With primary sources, teachers can easily answer the question, "So what?"

Ideas for using the following primary sources are provided on pages 81–87:

- Photographs
- Posters
- Cartoons
- Maps
- Artifacts
- Sound Recordings
- Film Recordings

Ideas for Using Primary Sources

Photographs

Visuals such as photographs help us to understand the past. Have your students consider looking through their own family photograph albums. This serves as a perfect opportunity to have students intimately connect with their own pasts.

Let's say that you have some of the harrowing photographs taken in the aftermath of the Battle of Antietam, September 17, 1862, accessible for your students. These photographs are not only important because of the carnage that they document, but they are important in how they shaped people's images and opinions of the Civil War. Students need to know that photographs not only record history, but that they can often shape history. A case in point here would be to consider some photographs of more recent vintage such as from the Vietnam War. Many photographs of that conflict shown in newspapers or magazines had a direct bearing on the perceptions and opinions of people who saw them.

Once you provide students with the photographs, have students study them for two minutes and then respond to the following:

- What are the students' overall impressions of the photograph?
- Divide the photograph into quadrants and study each quadrant in depth. What new details become visible?
- List all the people, objects, and activities in the photograph.
- Based on their observations, have students draw inferences from the photograph.
- List questions that are raised in their minds relative to the photograph.
- Where might students find answers to those questions?

Posters

Posters are another interesting way to learn about the past. Think about all the posters that were used on the home front in the United States during World War I and World War II or the posters expressing dissent during the Vietnam era.

Generally, effective posters use symbols that are unusual, simple, and direct. When studying posters, query students as to the impact of the poster that they are observing.

- Observe and list the main colors used in the poster.
- Determine what symbols, if any, are used in the poster.
- Are the symbols clear (easy to interpret), memorable, and/or dramatic?
- Explore the message in the poster. Is it primarily visual, verbal, or both?
- Determine the creator of the poster. Is the source of the poster a government agency, a non-profit organization, a special interest group, or a for-profit company?
- Define the intended audience for the poster and what response the creator of the poster was hoping to achieve.
- What purpose does the poster serve?

Excerpted from *Exploring History Through Primary Sources: The Great Depression* by Wendy Conklin. Copyright © 2003 by Teacher Created Materials, Inc.

Cartoons

Two other kinds of visuals that you can use to study history are political cartoons and cartoon strips. Many teachers use political cartoons to teach, but keep in mind that cartoon strips can also provide clues as to the tenor of the times. Since cartoons are drawn with the intent to send a message, you and your students should examine cartoons on three levels. The following can be done using political cartoons or cartoon strips.

Level One

- List the objects or people seen in the cartoon.
- Identify the cartoon caption and/or title.
- Locate words or phrases used by the cartoonist to identify objects or people within the cartoon.
- Record any important dates or numbers that appear in the cartoon.

Level Two

- Which of the objects on the list from level one are symbols?
- What is the meaning of each symbol?
- Which words or phrases in the cartoon appear to be most significant, and why?
- List some adjectives that describe the emotions or values portrayed or depicted in the cartoon.

Level Three

- Describe the action that is taking place in the cartoon.
- Explain how the words in the cartoon clarify the symbols.
- Explain the message of the cartoon.
- Determine which special interest groups, within the proper historical context, would agree and/or disagree with the cartoon's message. Why?

A REAL CHORE.

The G. O. P.—Well, I've Got That Panama Canal to Dig.
The Dem. Donk.—That's Nothin'! I Got to Dig Up an Issue.

"A Real Chore" from the Cleveland Journal

Maps

Historians of all kinds work with maps. Military historians use maps of particular battlefields to chart troop movements and analyze commander tactics. Social historians study maps of properties such as the homes and farms of homesteaders during the westward movement. How could one possibly study the route of Lewis and Clark through the Louisiana Territory along the Missouri River without the aid of a regional map? Better yet, study a facsimile of one of the many maps Lewis and Clark drew freehand as they moved across the uncharted terrain. Those historians who trace the migration patterns of people use all kinds of different maps as part of their study. Regardless, history, for the most part, happens on the surface of Earth and using maps can provide clues to place an event within its proper historical context.

As with other primary sources, there is a kind of process students should follow as part of their analysis and interpretation. Have the students decide what kind of map they are studying:

- raised relief map
- topographic map
- political map
- contour-line map
- natural resource map
- military map
- bird's-eye view map
- artifact map
- satellite photograph
- pictograph
- weather map
- another type of map

Examine the physical qualities of the map.

- Is there some kind of compass use related to the map? Describe it.
- Is the map handwritten or drawn?
- What dates, if any, are on the map?
- Are there any notations on the map? What are they?
- What is the scale of the map?
- Is the name of the mapmaker on the map? Who is it?
- Is there a title on the map? What is it?
- Can a legend or key be found on the map? Describe it.

Once determined, all of these clues about the map will help you to assist your students in keeping everything within the proper historical context. Finally, as part of your investigation of history using maps, have the students complete the following information about the map.

- List three things on the map that are important.
- Why was the map drawn or created?
- What evidence on the map suggests why it was drawn or created?
- Does the information on this map support or contradict information that students have read about this event? Explain.
- Write a question to the mapmaker that is left unanswered by this map.

Artifacts

Not only do historians use textual documents to study the past, but they also use artifacts, more properly called objects of material culture, in studying the lives of people or events of the past. It is much easier to grasp the reality of persons or events that have lived or gone on before us if we can look at, or better yet, hold something that is intimately connected to that person or event. Some wonderful examples are Theodore Roosevelt's glasses, one of Jacqueline Kennedy's formal evening gloves, an American Indian clay pot, the articles in Abraham Lincoln's pocket when he was shot, or a sign from a southern railway station clearly marking "White" or "Colored" restrooms or water fountains.

Again, when making this kind of inquiry with your students, it is important that they observe the physical qualities of the objects with which they are working. Students should first describe the material from which the object was made. Which of the following substances best describes the material?

- bone
- pottery
- wood
- metal
- stone
- leather

- glass
- paper
- cardboard
- cotton
- plastic
- some other material

Describe how the object looks and feels by describing its:

- shape
- color
- texture
- size

- weight
- movable parts
- items printed, stamped, or written on it

Finally, wrap up your work using the object you are studying by answering the following questions:

- For what might the object have been used?
- Who might have used it?
- When might it have been used?
- What does the artifact tell us?
- What does it tell us about the technology of the time in which it was made or used?
- What does it tell us about the life and times of the people who made it and used it?

A fun closure to your artifact observation might be to have students name a similar item today. Then, they can bring in a photograph, sketch, or the actual artifact. Students could also consider what artifacts we are creating today that might be studied in-depth in the future. What will these artifacts tell historians about us?

Sound Recordings

In the 20th century, society was able to record its voices and sounds through the genius of the work of Thomas Edison. Now, we can "hear" the sounds of the past through sound recordings. It's much better to listen to a recording of the October 1938 radio broadcast of Orson Welles and the Mercury Theater on the Air's production of the "War of the Worlds" than to just tell students about it. When studying the Great Depression, think how much more effective your instruction will be if your students can listen to President Franklin Roosevelt deliver one of his memorable "fireside chats." In some ways this is like time travel. As with the other primary sources discussed here, there are some steps to using sound recordings effectively with your students.

Pre-Listening Activity

- Based on the title alone, whose voice do the students think they will hear on this recording?
- What is the date of this recording?
- Where was the recording made?

Active-Listening Activity

- Decide the type of sound recording to which they are listening:
    - policy speech
    - congressional testimony
    - news report
    - interview
    - entertainment broadcast
    - press conference
    - convention proceedings
    - campaign speech
    - arguments before a court
    - panel discussion
    - another sound recording

- Students should also make note of the unique qualities of the recording (where applicable). Do they hear any of the following: music, narration, special sound effects, or background sounds?
- Was what they heard recorded in a studio, or was it a live broadcast?
- What was the tone or mood of this recording?

Post-Listening Activity

As part of student assessment of the recording, they should respond to the following:

- List three things in this sound recording that are important.
- Why was the original broadcast made and for what audience?
- What evidence in the recording helps students know why it was made?
- List two things this sound recording tells about life at the time it was made.
- How would you compare this recording with those of today?
- Write a question to the broadcaster that is left unanswered by this sound recording.
- What information is gained about this event or person that would not be conveyed by a written transcript of the recording? Be specific.

Film Recordings

While most people today do not write letters or keep diaries like they used to, historians of the future will have a tremendous amount of film recording to rely on when conducting their investigations. Increasingly, films of all kinds are being used to study and analyze what has transpired since the "Wizard of Menlo Park," Thomas Edison, created motion pictures. Like sound recordings, it is much easier to convey the history of a particular period, person, or event if one can study motion pictures directly related to that event. Students learn about the Japanese bombing of Pearl Harbor more effectively if they see the stark film footage that captured that "Day of Infamy." The August 1963 March on Washington for Jobs and Freedom takes on greater resonance and meaning when one can see and hear Martin Luther King, Jr., deliver his "I Have a Dream" speech. Watching King's facial expressions and body language, combined with the inflections of his voice, provides a kind of historic palpability that one cannot feel when simply reading King's words. The moment becomes transcendent.

Again, here are some simple tips to follow, providing you and your students with wide latitude in using films or motion pictures to make historic inquiries. Using this material, you will find that not only will students come away from the activity with a better sense of history, but also that they will have increased their media literacy.

Pre-Viewing Activity

- Either tell or have students determine the title of the film.
- Either tell or have students determine the source of the film.
- Based on the previous information, ask the students to suggest what they might see in this motion picture.
- Have the students list three concepts, ideas, or people that they might expect to see as they watch the film.

Active-Viewing Activity

- Ask students to determine whether or not the film is a(n):
  - animated cartoon
  - documentary film
  - newsreel
  - propaganda film
  - theatrical short subject
  - training film
  - combat film
  - other (if so, what type of film?)

- As part of student assessment of the film, they should respond to the following regarding the qualities of the motion picture. Does the film contain:
  - music
  - narration
  - special effects
  - color
  - live action
  - background noise
  - animation
  - dramatizations
  - other (if so, what?)

Excerpted from *Exploring History Through Primary Sources: The Great Depression* by Wendy Conklin. Copyright © 2003 by Teacher Created Materials, Inc.

Film Recordings *(cont.)*

- Be certain that students note how camera angles, lighting, music, narration, and/or editing contribute to creating an atmosphere in the film.
- Ask students to identify the tone or mood of the film.

Post-Viewing Activity

Immediately after viewing the film, have students circle the things that they listed in number four of the pre-viewing activity that they found in the film. Next, check their learning from the film using the following questions for assessment:

- What is the central message(s) of this motion picture?
- Consider the effectiveness of the film in communicating its message. As a tool of communication, what are its strengths and weaknesses?
- How do the students think the filmmakers wanted the audience to respond?
- Does the film appeal to the viewer's reason or emotion? How does it make the students feel?
- List two things this motion picture tells about life at the time it was made.
- Write a question to the filmmaker that is left unanswered by the motion picture.
- What information is gained about this event or person that would not be conveyed by a written source? Be specific.

Chapter 5 Review

1. Which of the following are examples of primary sources? (circle all that apply)

    a. letters

    b. diary entries

    c. photographs

    d. clothing

2. Why are primary sources an excellent way of teaching history? (circle all that apply)

    a. students like to see pictures of old things

    b. it gets students involved in the constructive process of history

    c. it provides relevance and meaning

3. When students understand the background of primary sources, they begin to _____. (circle all that apply)

    a. put historical events and attitudes into perspective

    b. think progressively

    c. walk in the shoes of their ancestors

    d. none of the above

4. True or False? The only way to get students to analyze a primary source photograph is to tell them to look at it.

Chapter 6 Pre-Reading Reflection

1. What is a simulation?

   _____

   _____

   _____

   _____

   _____

2. How can simulations enhance the learning process?

   _____

   _____

   _____

   _____

3. How does active learning equal authentic learning?

   _____

   _____

   _____

   _____

Simulations

What do you remember most about your experiences in school? How did you learn about the different subjects? Were you out of your seat and active? For example, did your teacher have you simply read a chapter on the Renaissance and then take a multiple-choice test? Or did you enter class one day to find yourself in a town council meeting in Florence? Your teacher convenes a meeting to decide where a piece of artwork created by the local artist, Michelangelo, should be placed. After viewing a picture of the statue named *David*, you and many others give ideas of where this statue would best suit the town. Unknown to you, the teacher has arranged with one student to reply with a planned answer. At the end of the discussion, that student raises his/her hand and says that it should be placed in the back corner of the loggia, an open air stage with columns, where no one can see it. The teacher asks that person his name, and he replies, "Leonardo da Vinci."

What an impression this simulation would make on the class! Instead of merely reading that there were antagonistic feelings between these two artists, students are allowed to participate in an event that actually took place in Florence. Will students remember this simulation? Students are more likely to remember a simulation in which they participated rather than remembering a text that they just read. This is active learning. And active learning is *authentic learning*.

What Are Simulations?

Simulations are activities that get students actively participating in the learning process. Some simulations demand that students involve their entire body. For example, in language arts, teachers can have students act out punctuation. When the teacher reads a sentence, students can show what the end punctuation should be by either curling into a ball on the floor for a period, jumping straight up and down for an exclamation point, or hunching their shoulders for a question mark.

Math teachers can employ the same concept for adding, subtracting, multiplying, or dividing. Put students into groups and have them form their bodies into the number that answers a math sentence. For example, the teacher might ask groups to solve five times five. Each group will need to use their bodies to show that the answer is 25.

A science teacher might use a simulation to show how warm and cold molecules differ in their activity. The teacher will need to mark off a small square area in a room and then tell the students to be molecules. Students should walk inside the square area very slowly without touching anyone. As students are doing this, explain that cold molecules act this way. They live comfortably in small tight areas. That is why cold air sinks. Then tell students to walk around very fast inside the square area. They will be bumping into each other. As students are doing this, explain that warm molecules act this way. Their activity has increased and so they need more space to keep from bumping into each other. They need to expand and that is why warm air rises. All these simulations engage students actively.

In other simulations, students visualize themselves in another time period or situation. These types of activities lend themselves easily to historical events. Simulations can provide students the opportunity to travel back in time, think like the people did back then, discuss strategies, and make decisions as if they were a part of the actual historic event. In this book, there is a distinction made between simulations and problem-based learning. While some simulations have students solving problems and working toward conclusions, the ultimate goal for a simulation is that students *experience* the simulation. The goal for problem-based learning is for students to *solve* a problem. (Problem-based learning was explored in Chapter 4.)

Simulations vary in length and commitment. Depending on the topic and the amount of time that can be devoted to a simulation, they can be very simple and quick or very involved and last several hours, days, or weeks.

The simulation between Michelangelo and da Vinci only takes a few minutes and would serve as a great opener to a unit of study. A simulation involving passengers aboard the *Santa Maria, Niña,* and *Pinta* could take several days and help students to understand what it would have been like to travel with Columbus on a ship. Students can be a citizen accused of witchcraft during the Salem witch trials and decide how they will plead. A simulation between the North and the South during the Civil War could take weeks and would help students understand the intense issues that divided a nation and caused a war. A section of the students in the classroom can be quarantined during a study of World War II to show what it was like to be a Japanese American living in the United States.

Why Use Simulations?

Research shows that facts are more likely to be recalled if emotions are tapped right after a learning experience (McGaugh et al., 1995). When students participate in simulations, they actively participate in learning. When simulations are used, the emotions are engaged in the learning process. Experiences generate emotions, which allows students to express opinions.

Research also suggests that that there are significant links between learning and body movements (Jensen, 1998). Because of this link, it is imperative that teachers integrate movement into learning everyday. Simulations are a great way to involve movement while learning.

Through simulations, students can learn the history of the time period and learn to think like the people did during that time period. They begin to understand why people made particular decisions, and they offer ideas for what could have been done differently. When students encounter learning like this, they remember better what was taught. For example, Edgar Allan Poe wrote the genre that he did because of the time in which he lived. What did Mark Twain's childhood have to do with the books that he wrote? It's important to understand Shakespeare's time frame in order to fully understand his writings.

These types of activities pack a lot of exciting content and details into a short amount of time. Simulations teach what textbooks teach, but the format provides a more exciting learning environment. Students get excited about history and it suddenly becomes meaningful because their emotions are involved.

Simulations challenge students to use higher-level thinking skills. It provides interaction and feedback, something textbooks cannot do, and students evaluate history in the process.

Ideas for Using Simulations

First of all, when a simulation is finished, students should always compare the simulated event with the actual event. How are they alike and how are they different? Teachers need to assist students in analyzing these two events. Students could simulate important historical events from any curriculum area, such as Social Studies, Science, Math, Literature, and Art. The following are a few examples of simulations and activities you could use in your classroom. For more discussion and activity ideas on these and other simulations, see *Social Studies Strategies for Active Learning* by Dr. Andi Stix (2004).

Bartering

Bartering is a fun activity that turns the classroom into a babble of hagglers, traders, and bargain hunters, and in the process gives students an opportunity to learn the strengths and weaknesses of exchanging goods without using money. Students become members of a self-sufficient community, whether in ancient Egypt, ancient Greece, or as European peasants of the Middle Ages (Stix, 2004).

Sample Activity: Bartering in Colonial America

In this activity, students simulate a day at a marketplace in Colonial America. The object is for each student to trade away his/her items and to accumulate a variety of other goods for his/her family. Have students keep a simple bartering ledger so that they can review their trades and determine whether or not they had a good bartering day.

1. Divide students into equal groups—each group can represent a different colonial settlement. Try to include colonies from the New England Colonies, (Plymouth, Massachusetts Bay, etc.), the Middle Colonies (New Amsterdam, New Netherlands, etc.), and the Southern Colonies (Jamestown, Charleston, etc.).

2. Distribute labels for students to wear with different colonial occupations, such as butcher, farmer, dairy farmer, baker, leather maker and shoe weaver, weaver, glazier/glass blower, and carpenter. Assign each student in a group a different occupation.

3. Distribute cards with possible items that were traded in Colonial America, such as corn, maple syrup, dairy, leather goods, metal ware, fruit, and meat. Be sure that each occupation has an equal number of items for bartering. In each group, have students make piles of their cards, i.e., the farmer places all tomato cards together in one pile, all apples into another pile, etc.

4. Model the activity before you proceed. Walk up to a "concession stand" and browse through the cards. Tell the person that you'd like to barter. This person then browses through your cards. The person tells you what he/she would like, and you reply by stating what you'd like. You negotiate together to determine how many cards of theirs would be an equitable trade with yours. For example, a chair that was cut and carved from raw wood can never be worth the same amount as a dozen apples. Once you agree, you exchange cards. Have students continue independently, keeping track of their trades in their bartering ledgers.

Excerpted from *Exploring History: Colonial America* by Dr. Andi Stix and Frank Hrbek. Copyright © 2001 by Teacher Created Materials, Inc.

Lobbyist Hearing

In this simulation, students simulate participating in a public meeting, where panel members listen to the persuasive opinions of different interest groups to determine an important decision. The interest groups try to persuade a panel to their point of view about what should be done. The panel can act the part of judges, legislators, or congressmen and women (Stix, 2004).

Sample Activity: Should or Shouldn't We Celebrate Columbus Day?

In this activity, students will simulate a congressional committee hearing to determine whether or not the United States should celebrate Columbus Day.

1. Separate the class into a maximum of five lobbyist groups and assign each group one of the following points of view, which they will use to argue for or against Columbus Day. Have students research their assigned point of view with their groups or individually.

Points of View

- Cheng Ho, a great Chinese explorer who voyaged all over Southeast Asia
- Scandinavian Vikings, who sailed the oceans prior to Columbus
- Native Americans, such as the Carib Indians from the Caribbean Islands, who had lived in the New World for many years
- Christopher Columbus, explorer in search of a new all-water route to Asia
- Vasco de Gama, the Portuguese explorer, who discovered the all-water route around Africa to India

---

2. In their lobbyist groups, students generate a list of key issues to argue their viewpoint. Each student must choose one or two points from the list to write his/her own 30-second to one-minute speech.

3. As students write and practice their speeches, pull one student from each group to form the panel that will make the final decision (make sure it is an odd number). These panel members must now create a list of questions that they want answered by the lobbyists before making their decision.

4. Call on one lobbying group at a time—the first speaker states the group's point of view and whether it is for or against the issue. After each member's speech, each panel member asks at least one follow-up question of the group. Repeat with each lobbyist group.

5. After some discussion, the committee makes its decision and announces it to the class. Allow for discussion on the entire process as a whole-class follow-up.

Excerpted from *Exploring History: The Age of Exploration* by Dr. Andi Stix and Frank Hrbek. Copyright © 2000 by Teacher Created Materials, Inc.

Vote On It!

This is an activity in which students participate in the task of determining leadership qualities by examining the résumés of people from a specific time period. The names of the individuals are omitted from the résumés, and the goal is to help select one of the people to complete a given job, i.e., help President Lincoln choose a new general to lead the northern armies during the Civil War. Students will choose the individual they feel is best qualified by his or her education, experience, and background (Stix, 2004).

Sample Activity: Elect the First President of the United States

In this activity, students are given the résumés of candidates who lived during the American Revolution. Students must choose the candidate they think would make the greatest contribution to the leadership of the United States.

1. Divide the class into cooperative groups of four students. Ask each student to first generate independently a list of qualifications he/she would like to see in a presidential candidate. Each student then shares his/her ideas with the group, and they collectively decide on their top ten priorities.

2. Create résumé cards for notable historical individuals from the American Revolution and randomly number them. Distribute one set of four to six résumé cards to each pair of students. The following is George Washington's résumé:

> H   **Education:** No formal education   H
>
> **Work Experience:** Farmer; land surveyor; planter; military officer and commander-in-chief; member of a lawmaking body; congressional member; land investor; justice of the peace
>
> **Personal Background:** Married, has stepchildren, adopted two of his grandchildren
>
> H   **Age as of 1789:** 57   H

3. Students read the résumés and compare and contrast the data about the six unknown candidates. A vote is held within each group, and the majority selection wins as if the Electoral College had met. Discuss the reasons each group voted for a particular candidate and then reveal each candidate's identity. Students will be surprised by some of their choices!

Flexogeneous Reading Groups

For this strategy, teachers can prepare readings that are nonfiction, based on primary source documents, such as newspaper clippings, biographies, and magazine articles. At first, each member of a cooperative learning group of students receives the same reading, which differs from another group. They discuss the piece in depth. Then, they are "jigsawed" into new groups, which bring together members who represent different readings. Another variation of this strategy is to use historical fiction or historical young-adult literature written at varying reading levels, which allow for student choice, differentiation, and the discussion on a specific book (Stix, 2004).

Sample Activity: Literature Circles and Journal Writing

Literature Circles: If you have 24 students in your classroom, you could offer four different books to students—novels written with slightly different focuses during any specific historical period. The first step is to group students by book and to assign a specific number of pages to be read. Ask students one open-ended question before they are given the reading assignment—it will be the same for all groups. Pose questions such as these:

- Describe how the environment is having an effect on the main character.
- Describe the tensions between the main character and other characters in the book.
- In what ways is the setting described in your book different from your hometown or city?
- Describe what is happening historically that creates tension within the story.
- If you were living back in that historical time period, what would you find most disturbing and want to change?

When students return to class, have them sit with their groups and discuss their answers to the question posed. The second level is to "jigsaw" students into new groups, so that students who read different books are represented in the new groups. Students discuss the same question. Their common bond is the time and main historical events of each book.

Journal writing: Have each student keep a journal. Encourage students to use multimodal journal writing, where they can write, draft diagrams, draw pictures, design and draw tables of simple statistics, or even paste pictures of small collectibles onto the pages. Allow them to reflect in their journals after each literature circle.

Excerpted from *Social Studies Strategies for Active Learning* by Dr. Andi Stix. Copyright © 2004 by Teacher Created Materials, Inc.

Playlets

Students fashion the dialogues and settings as they write their own scripts. They may elect to do a puppet show, interview, jury trial, musical, poetry that utilizes rhyme, flashback technique, live comic strip, regular drama, or some other format that the students design. This strategy is best suited to periods in history that encompass a decade or two, the administration of a powerful president or leader, sections of a long story, or any event that had cataclysmic results (Stix, 2004).

Sample Activity: The Rosetta Stone Skits

In this activity, students will write their own two- to three-page script of a scene from the Rosetta Stone story.

1. Create scene cards that cover different stages of the Rosetta Stone story. In addition to the sample scenes on page 101, you could also create scene cards for the following events (create them yourself or have students create them as a whole-class project):
   - The French start to decipher the Rosetta Stone
   - The French begin their quest in deciphering the Rosetta Stone
   - The British make the Rosetta Stone available for their scholars
   - Dr. Thomas Young tries to decipher the Rosetta Stone
   - Champollion's early investigations
   - Champollion examines Alexander the Great's cartouche

2. Using a sentence from one of the scene cards on page 101, set the stage by modeling how to write a historical fiction script with historical fiction characters.

3. Divide students into cooperative groups of four to five students and assign one scene per group, providing copies of the cards for each student. It is essential that all students have a part. Ask students to discuss the points of their scenes before they begin writing their scripts. Allow the students time to edit their work, rehearse, and bring in props. They could also incorporate graphics, maps, and artifacts to embellish their scripts and to make them livelier.

4. Provide enough class time for each group to act out its skit. After each performance, a question-and-answer period should be allowed.

Excerpted from *Exploring History: Ancient Egypt* by Dr. Andi Stix and Frank Hrbek. Copyright © 2004 by Teacher Created Materials, Inc.

Rosetta Stone Scenes

A PACKAGE IS SENT FROM ROSETTA, EGYPT

In late August, a large, heavy package was delivered to the headquarters of the French scholars and scientists in Cairo; it was sent by a young French military engineer named Pierre-Francois-Xavier Bouchard.

It contained a black basalt stone slab inscribed with the writing of three different languages; the stone measured 3 feet 9 inches by 2 feet 4¼ inches (115 cm x 72 cm).

A message was sent with the package from the French army officer that stated that when soldiers were tearing down a ruined wall in a fort near the town of Rosetta, 35 miles (56 km) north of Alexandria, they unearthed (discovered) a section containing this slab. The only corner left was the lower left side, and the officer stated that the men tried to find the missing pieces but had no luck.

The scholars labeled the stone slab the "Rosetta Stone" in tribute to where it was found; today that town is known as Rashid.

THE FRENCH ARE FORCED TO GIVE UP THE ROSETTA STONE IN EGYPT

Two years later, in the spring of 1801, the British landed troops in Egypt, the Turks had re-conquered Cairo, and the French were forced to retreat to Alexandria.

General Hutchinson, the British commander, insisted that all research material collected by the French scholars and scientists be handed over to the British.

General Menou, commanding the French troops, wanted to keep the Rosetta stone. The French scholars protested, saying, *"Without us, this material is a dead language that neither you nor your scientists can understand."* General Menou even tried to claim the stela slab as his own property.

While the British allowed the scholars to keep the majority of what they found and their interpretations, they stubbornly insisted on taking the Rosetta stone.

Acting with remarkable quickness, General Menou was smart enough to lay printer's ink on the stone, lay a sheet of paper on it, pressing rubber rollers over it to get a good, clear impression.

General Menou gave in finally and turned to General Hutchinson and said, *"You can have it, because you are the stronger of us two."*

Excerpted from *Exploring History: Ancient Egypt* by Dr. Andi Stix and Frank Hrbek. Copyright © 2004 by Teacher Created Materials, Inc.

Chapter 6 Review

1. True or False? Students should never compare the simulated event with the actual event.

2. Which of the following are true about simulations?

   a. They challenge students to use higher-level thinking skills.

   b. They provide interaction and feedback.

   c. They have students evaluate history.

   d. All of the above

3. Research also suggests that _____.

   a. there are significant links between learning and body movements

   b. facts are more likely to be recalled if emotions are used right after a learning experience

   c. both a and b

   d. None of the above

4. True or False? The ultimate goal for a simulation experience is for students to handle and analyze primary source materials.

Chapter 7 Pre-Reading Reflection

1. What are some of the different ways that you think students learn?

   _____

   _____

   _____

   _____

2. Why is it important to consider what kind of learners students are when planning your curriculum?

   _____

   _____

   _____

   _____

3. According to Gardner's theory, we all have strengths in certain intelligences and weaknesses in others. How can weak areas be developed?

   _____

   _____

   _____

   _____

Multiple Intelligences

"It's not how smart you are, but how you are smart."
—René Diaz-Lefebrve

Teachers across the nation are repeatedly finding it challenging to teach the new generation of students who demand constant entertainment. Television, music videos, and especially computer games are just the tip of the iceberg when listing what preoccupies students' minds. How can schools possibly compete with this mirage of fast and entertaining information? Do we as educators cave in to the habits of bribing and entertaining students in the hopes of keeping their attention? What is the secret to increasing students' confidence, helping them become self-directed learners, and thus instilling the love of learning? If we merely bribe and entertain students, we are only feeding the problem, and it will worsen. Instead, we should offer students activities that engage their natural talents and gifts.

How can we find out their natural talents and gifts? Understanding your students is the first step in being able to do this. What makes them tick? What do they enjoy? How do they learn best? How do your students best express what they know?

Just in the past few years, researchers have provided various ways to understand students. One way is to build lesson plans around the model of *Multiple Intelligences.* This model seeks to nurture the broad range of talents in students. It identifies and categorizes eight different intelligences. Today, this information is readily available to teachers who can use this information to create curriculum that nurtures these intelligences in students.

What Are Multiple Intelligences?

The multiple intelligence model is based on the work of one primary researcher named Howard Gardner. He has identified eight intelligences, which include verbal/linguistic; logical/mathematical; bodily/kinesthetic; intrapersonal; interpersonal; musical/rhythmic; visual/spatial; and naturalistic. Researchers say that everyone possesses each of these intelligences, but some intelligences are more developed than others.

In most classrooms, intelligence is measured logically/mathematically and verbally/linguistically. But some teachers are finding that Gardner's theory of multiple intelligences is like a breath of fresh air. Teachers who learn about this theory finally begin to understand why they teach the way they do. The tendency is to teach according to one's own intelligence preference (Gardner, 1993).

Here is a quick review of the eight intelligences:

Musical/Rhythmic Intelligence—the ability to recognize and compose musical tones, rhythms, and pitches. Generally, these people like to sing, play an instrument, hum tunes, compose music, and listen to music. They are good at remembering melodies and noticing sounds. They learn best when there is rhythm, melody, and/or music associated with learning.

Visual/Spatial Intelligence—the ability to create mental images and pictures in order to solve problems. These individuals generally like to draw, design, build, day-dream, do art projects, create architecture, and watch videos. They are good at visual imagery, mazes, puzzles, reading charts, maps, and other graphic organizers. They learn best when they can visualize, dream, and work with color, pictures, and graphic representations of information.

Bodily/Kinesthetic Intelligence—the ability to use movement for learning. These people like to touch, talk, use body language, and move around. They are usually good at physical activities like acting, athletics, and dance. They learn best with "hands on" activities where they can touch and move, processing through bodily senses.

Verbal/Linguistic Intelligence—involves expertise with language. People strong in the verbal/linguistic intelligence can express themselves well rhetorically and can use language as a means to remember information. Generally, they like to read, write, and tell stories. They tend to be good at memorizing names, places, and dates. They learn best when they say, hear, or see words.

Logical/Mathematical Intelligence—involves reasoning deductively and thinking logically. This intelligence is generally associated with scientific and mathematical thinking. People strong in logical/mathematical intelligence like to work with numbers, explore patterns, do experiments, and solve problems. They are typically good at math, reasoning, problem solving, and logic. They learn best when they can sequence, categorize, classify, and work with patterns and numbers.

Interpersonal Intelligence—the ability to understand the feelings and intentions of others. Generally, these people have lots of friends and enjoy joining groups and talking to others. They are good at understanding people, solving conflicts, teaching, management, and are often leaders. They learn best when they are allowed to share, relate, and cooperate with others.

Intrapersonal Intelligence—the ability to understand one's own feelings and motivations. Generally, these people like to work alone and pursue their own interests. They are good at understanding themselves, psychology, counseling, and tend to be goal-oriented. They learn best on their own with individualized projects and self-paced instruction.

Naturalist Intelligence—the ability to classify natural phenomena and have an ongoing curiosity and knowledge of the natural world. Generally, these people love to be outdoors. They are good with natural history, plants, and animals. They learn best when they can go outside and explore in nature's classroom.

Why Use Multiple Intelligences?

The reason why so many educators love the multiple intelligence model best is because it is a flexible way of designing curriculum and creating learning environments. It gives a basic framework for each of the eight intelligences, and then teachers form their own unique lesson plans around it, providing various learning experiences for their students.

Many educators have come to think of multiple intelligences as a philosophy of how children learn. It provides avenues by which all students can achieve success. Sue Teele from the University of California, Riverside sums up Gardner's goal of the multiple intelligence model by saying that "multiple intelligences provides for different windows into the same room. We need to unleash the creative potential in all our schools in order to open as many windows as possible for every student in every classroom to succeed." She concludes by emphasizing that "the future mandates that we all move forward together in a way that builds on both our mutual strengths and respects our unique differences" (Teele, 1994, p. 17).

Howard Gardner believes that students possess all eight of the multiple intelligences. Some are just better developed than others. Teachers can use multiple intelligences as a strategy that challenges students to take control of their own learning. When students understand how they learn best, they will also understand their weaknesses. While it is good to have activities that enhance students' natural talents, teachers can also use the information about each student to encourage him/her to develop his/her weak intelligences. More often than not, students will take on this responsibility and work toward developing their weak intelligences.

Certain schools that have adopted the multiple intelligence model schoolwide have reported a rise in standardized test scores. Studies conducted by Linda and Bruce Campbell (1999) in six schools, ranging from elementary to high school, have shown an increase in standardized test scores. These schools are in various locations all over the country and range demographically, from inner city to suburban, magnet schools to public schools, low-class to middle- and upper-class neighborhoods, and low population of minority students to a high population of minority students.

Some research suggests that certain pathways of learning are stronger at certain stages of development. Sue Teele (1994) devised a survey titled the "Teele Inventory for Multiple Intelligences" (TIMI). She gave it to over 6,000 students. Her research found that verbal/linguistic intelligence is strongest in kindergarten through third grade. It declines dramatically thereafter. The logical/mathematical intelligence is strongest in first through fourth grade. It also declines dramatically thereafter. The visual/spatial and bodily/kinesthetic intelligence was shown to be dominant throughout elementary and middle school. In addition, middle school children also show a preference for musical/rhythmic and interpersonal intelligences.

What does Teele's information mean? It means that if elementary teachers want to use the best strategies, they must present lessons that incorporate verbal/linguistic, logical/mathematical, visual/spatial, and bodily/kinesthetic activities. If middle school teachers want to use the best strategies, they must present lessons that incorporate visual/spatial, bodily/kinesthetic, musical/rhythmic, and interpersonal activities. Sadly, in many classrooms, the middle school teacher instructs with lectures and mere readings of texts. This is exactly opposite of how middle school students learn best. For a general overview of Teele's findings, see Figure 7.1 on page 111.

The lists on pages 112 and 113 provide ideas for products for the multiple intelligences.

Figure 7.1: Dominant Strengths by Grade Level

	Picture Smart (Visual/spatial)	Word Smart (Verbal/linguistic)	Body Smart (Bodily/kinesthetic)	Self Smart (Intrapersonal)	People Smart (Interpersonal)	Music Smart (Musical/rhythmic)	Number Smart (Logical/Mathematical)
Kindergarten	✗	✗	✗	✗			✗
First grade	✗	✗	✗				✗
Second grade	✗	✗	✗				✗
Third grade	✗	✗	✗		✗		✗
Fourth grade	✗		✗		✗	✗	✗
Fifth grade	✗		✗		✗	✗	
Sixth grade	✗		✗		✗	✗	
Middle school	✗		✗		✗	✗	
High school	✗		✗		✗	✗	

Printed by permission from Sue Teele.

Products For Multiple Intelligences

A dance/a letter/a lesson
Advertisement
Animated movie
Annotated bibliography
Art gallery
Block picture story
Bulletin board
Bumper sticker
Chart
Choral reading
Clay sculpture
Code
Collage
Collection
Comic strip
Computer program
Costumes
Crossword puzzle
Database
Debate
Demonstration
Detailed illustration
Diorama
Diary
Display
Edibles
Editorial essay
Etching
Experiment
Fact tile
Fairy tale
Family tree
Fiction story
Film
Filmstrip
Flip book

Game
Graph
Hidden Picture
Illustrated story
Interview
Jingle
Joke book
Journal
Labeled diagram
Large scale drawing
Learning center
Letter to the Editor
Map with legend
Mazes
Mobile
Model
Mosaic
Mural
Museum exhibit
Musical instruments
Needlework
Newspaper story
Non-fiction
Oral defense
Oral report
Painting
Pamphlet
Pantomime
Papier mache
Petition
Photo essay
Pictures
Picture story for children
Plaster of Paris model
Play
Poetry

Political cartoon
Pop-up book
Postage stamp
   (commemoratives)
Press conference
Project cube
Prototype
Puppet
Puppet show
Puzzle
Rap
Radio program
Rebus story
Recipe
Riddle
Role play
Science fiction story
Sculpture
Skit
Slide show
Slogan
Soliloquy
Song
Sound
Story telling—tall tales
Survey
Tapes–Audio–Video
Television program
Time line
Transparencies
Travel brochure
Venn diagram
Web homepage
Working hypothesis
Write a new law
Video film

Multiple Intelligences Product Grid

This product grid categorizes different products under separate headings according to research from Howard Gardner's multiple-intelligences theory. Many are listed in more than one column and would look different according to which approach is taken by the student. These groupings appeal to student interests and strengths. This increases the students' involvement and the quality of the final product. Having a final product makes it easier to determine that students have completed tasks that are measurable and demonstrable.

Verbal/Linguistic	Logical/Mathematical	Visual/Spatial	Bodily/Kinesthetic	Musical	Interpersonal	Intrapersonal	Naturalist
Advertisement	Advertisement	Animated movie	Calligraphy	Audio-video tape	Advertisement	Bulletin board	Artifact collecting
Annotated bibliography	Annotated bibliography	Art gallery	Charades	Choral reading	Animated movie	Chart	Diorama
Bulletin board	Chart	Bulletin board	Collage	Fairy tale	Bulletin board	Collection	Field study
Code	Code	Bumper sticker	Costumes	Film	Chart	Comic strip	Field trip
Comic strip	Collage	Cartoon	Dance	Instrumental	Choral reading	Diary	Fossil collecting
Debate	Collection	Chart	Demonstration	Jukebox	Comic strip	Editorial essay	Insect collecting
Demonstration	Computer program	Clay sculpture	Diorama	Musical	Debate	Fairy tale	Leaf collecting
Diary	Crossword puzzle	Collage	Etching	Poem	Demonstration	Family tree	Original song
Editorial essay	Database	Costumes	Experiment	Rap song	Editorial essay	Journal	Photo essay
Fairy tale	Debate	Demonstration	Film	Riddle	Fairy tale	Learning center	Rock collection
Family tree	Demonstration	Diorama	Flip book	Role playing	Film game	Poem	Scientific drawing
Fiction story	Detailed illustration	Display	Food	Song	Interview	Riddle maze collage	Spelunking trip
Interview	Edibles	Etching	Hidden picture	Sound	Journal	Time line	Time line
Jingle	Experiment	Film	Mosaic		Lesson		
Joke book	Fact tile	Filmstrip	Mural		Mazes		
Journal	Family tree	Flipbook	Musical		Museum exhibit		
Lesson	Game	Game	Musical instruments		Pamphlet		
Letter	Graph	Graph	Needlework		Petition		
Letter to the editor	Hidden picture	Hidden picture	Painting		Play		
Newspaper story	Labeled diagram	Illustrated story	Pantomime		Press conference		
Non-fiction	Large scale drawing	Maze	Papier mache		Role playing		
Oral defense	Lesson	Mobile	Plaster of Paris model		TV program		
Oral report	Map with legend	Model	Play				
Pamphlet	Mazes	Mosaic	Poem				
Petition	Mobile	Mural	Press conference				
Play	Model	Painting	Puppet				
Poem	Petition	Papier mache	Puppet show				
Press conference	Play	Photo essay	Radio program				
Radio program	Prototype	Picture story for children	Role play				
Riddle	Puzzle	Pictures	Transparencies				
Science fiction story	Recipe	Play	TV program				
Skit	Riddle	Political cartoon					
Slogan	Survey	Pop-up book					
Soliloquy	Time line	Prototype					
Story telling	Transparencies	Rebus story					
TV program	Venn diagram	Slide show					
Write a new law	Working hypothesis	Story cube					
	Write a new law	Transparencies					
		Travel brochure					
		TV program					
		Web home page					

Biology Lesson Ideas (Middle School Level)

Verbal/Linguistic—Any number of research projects like oral presentations, written projects/research papers, or poetry would fall under this domain. Students can select a part of the body (particular organ bones or muscular region) or a certain animal (microscopic, pets, or native), conduct research, and create a multimedia presentation, which is then shared with the class.

Visual/Spatial—Any biology-related art project would meet the needs of those who prefer this intelligence. This includes creating drawings, paintings, sculptures, collages, etc. If your students decide to prepare a multi-media presentation, they can use a drawing program on their computer. Otherwise students may prepare an oral presentation about the topic and draw a picture or complete an art project.

Bodily/Kinesthetic—Coordinate an outdoor game called "Survivor," which shows the predator/prey relationships among animals. Mark off an outdoor area. Assign students to be different animals—some herbivores and others carnivores. Students should know how the food cycle works in the animal kingdom, i.e. which animals eat other animals. The goal of the game is to collect the necessities of food and water while staying alive. If a player tags another player, that player "eats" them. The prey's food and water are passed on to its predator, and the prey is taken from the game area.

Musical/Rhythmic—Musically-inclined students could write a rap or song about one aspect of biology or create a song that uses body movements.

Interpersonal—Have students work in groups to complete one of these projects.

Naturalist—Assign students the task of classifying animals, learning the kingdom through species for an animal, and showing the relationships among animals (diagram).

Chapter 7 Review

1. People who learn best when they are outdoors exploring the world around them are strong in which of the following intelligences?

    a. interpersonal

    b. musical

    c. naturalist

    d. intrapersonal

2. Which of the following intelligences is most closely related to the ability to solve problems involving patterns?

    a. visual/spatial

    b. verbal/linguistic

    c. bodily/kinesthetic

    d. logical/mathematical

3. Which of the following intelligences is most closely associated with the ability to empathize with others?

    a. interpersonal

    b. musical

    c. naturalist

    d. intrapersonal

4. People whose abilities lie in visualizing and interpreting graphic representations such as maps and charts are said to be strong in this intelligence:

    a. musical/rhythmic

    b. verbal/linguistic

    c. visual/spatial

    d. logical/mathematical

Chapter 8 Pre-Reading Reflection

1. What benefit does movement have on learning?

   _____

   _____

   _____

   _____

   _____

2. What is one way you could integrate movement into a math lesson?

   _____

   _____

   _____

   _____

   _____

3. How can movement be infused in everyday activities?

   _____

   _____

   _____

   _____

Creative Dramatics

Have you ever led your students on an expedition to explore the inside of a human body? After they have washed their hands, have students imagine they are a piece of food. They must shrink down as small as they can, then step inside the mouth. Tell them to touch the tiny bumps on the tongue. Explain that they are touching the taste buds. Different taste buds are used to taste the sour, sweet, and salty foods we eat. Then have students count the teeth that they see. Does anyone know the names of these teeth? Move toward the throat and learn about how food is swallowed. Where does food go from there? This scenario can go on for a long time as the topic of the human body is studied.

As you see from this example, students are guided by their leader, who happens to be a teacher. The leader guides the students to imagine, enact, and reflect on this experience. This leader should have a great sense of humor and lots of energy. After all, he/she will lead students into the giant forest, through a snake-infested pit, and finally to the edge of the world! Their leader is facilitating language and communication skills, problem-solving skills, and creativity. In the process, students are developing a strong self concept, social awareness, and empathy. Does this type of activity have a name? Yes, it is called *creative dramatics*.

What Is Creative Dramatics?

To understand creative dramatics, it is first important to know what it is *not*. Creative dramatics is not an academic topic. It is not theater, either. With a children's theater, we have a published script to go by, beautiful scenery, and an audience. Creative dramatics needs none of these things. Creative dramatics is for the learner (or actor), not the audience. Creative dramatics is much more creative than merely staging and performing a play. There is no need for speaking, although speaking is not prohibited. Costumes are not necessary either. Everyone participates, not just the best actors and actresses. And it is not just for children. People of all ages can experience and benefit from creative dramatics. The goal is simply movement and imagination.

While there are no achievement tests and no behavioral objectives, it is also important to understand that creative dramatics does what traditional class work cannot do. "Creative imagination is worth more than mere book knowledge. Education and intelligence are merely the means by which we facilitate the liberation of this creative energy" (Davis, 1998, p. 272).

Creative dramatics is an effective learning tool that involves active learning experiences for students of all ages. It is a way to engage students' imagination. It is designed to strengthen problem solving, imagination, physical control, sensory awareness, self-confidence, humor, and awareness and understanding of others. It is structured, goal-oriented play.

Why Use Creative Dramatics?

Creative dramatics is a form of kinesthetic learning. Researcher James Hoetker says that drama accommodates visual and kinesthetic learners. Movement gets the blood flowing and, as a result, more oxygen is transported to the brain. When this happens, attention is increased. Students learn to control their physical bodies, their emotions, and their senses.

Creative dramatics helps students reframe what they already know into new perspectives and makes learning personal as students enter the imaginary world and take on imaginary roles. In addition, teachers report more instances of higher level thinking in their classrooms.

Creative dramatics stimulates problem solving, thinking, and imagination. The emphasis is on creativity, not performing. Drama also increases originality, fluency, and flexibility (Hoetker, 1969).

Furthermore, concentration and awareness are increased, as well as a sense of humor. Recent research says that humor in the classroom is beneficial to the learning process. It can increase retention anywhere from 15% to 50%. This happens because laughter causes more blood to be pumped to the brain. The brain releases endorphins (the chemicals that make a person feel good) in the bloodstream (Glenn, 2002).

Students develop a sense of pride and a strong self-confidence in performing and speaking. Most importantly, creative dramatics helps students to empathize with others around them (Way, 1967; Davis, Helfert, & Shapiro, 1973).

Finally, research done on the primary level has found that creative dramatics improves both reading comprehension and persuasive writing (Pellegrini & Galda, 1982; Gourgey, 1984; Wagner, 1987).

Creative Dramatics Stimulates:

Critical thinking

Creativity

Originality

Fluency

Flexibility

Imagination

Empathetic attitudes

Concentration

Physical control

Emotional control

Self-confidence

Sensory awareness

Problem solving

Elements of Language Learning While Using Creative Dramatics:

Making predictions

Using descriptive language

Asking questions

Comparing and contrasting

Drawing conclusions

Making judgments

Assessing cause and effect

Developing generalizations

Formulating and testing hypotheses

Ideas for Using Creative Dramatics

Vocal Exercises

Provide a sentence for students and then have them say it using different emotions, qualities, or as different characters, as shown in the box below. For example, students will say the sentence using a different type of voice inflection.

angry	painful	shaky	a mouse	a cow	a king
nasal-like	quiet	scared	mysterious	happy	bored
a monster	large	surprised	jealous	high voice	an adult voice
low voice	fast	loud	soft	nervous	a spoiled child's voice

Example: Introduce the sentence, "Are you going to wear that?" Have a student say it in a humorous voice. Then have another student say it in a scared voice. Another student can say it in a timid voice.

Other sentences to use:

1. There's an elephant in my bathtub.

2. The red coats are coming.

3. This classroom is a mess.

4. To be or not to be, that is the question.

Take a line from a popular song, a famous quote, a TV commercial, or a sentence with a new vocabulary word and try the exercise above.

Physical Drama Exercises

These are exercises for the body much like pantomime.

1. Walk like a bowl of cooked macaroni, a tiger, a bowl of gelatin, or a tree.

2. You see a lump under the rug that keeps moving. Take care of that lump.

3. Fix a bowl of ice cream with a can of sardines on top. Then eat it.

4. You are an ant under a picnic table. Find some food and take it home.

5. Paint a picture in the air for your teacher.

Developing Characters

Students can act out famous scenes from history, episodes from a book, and other scenarios.

1. You are Benjamin Franklin flying a kite in a lightning storm. Show how you discover electricity.

2. You are Bilbo Baggins and have encountered Gollum in the dark cave. Play both characters and show the audience how Gollum might have treated Bilbo if Gollum still had his magic ring.

3. The big-mouthed family is eating dinner. Show the audience what this looks like.

4. You are in the cafeteria when an Orc from the *Lord of the Rings* sees your ring. The Orc thinks it is the Ring of Power and wants it. Show the audience what happens.

Chapter 8 Review

1. True or False? Creative dramatics should only be used with young children.

2. Research says that humor in the classroom is beneficial to the learning process because _____.

   a. kids like to have a good time

   b. it can increase retention anywhere from 15% to 50%

   c. even teachers need to have a funny moment

   d. None of the above

3. Which of the following is true about creative dramatics?

   a. It is like children's theater.

   b. It uses props and costumes.

   c. It performs for an audience.

   d. None of the above

4. True or False? Creative dramatics strengthens problem solving, imagination, physical control, sensory awareness, self-confidence, humor, and awareness and understanding of others.

Chapter Reviews Answer Key

Chapter 1 Review (page 26)

  1. d

  2. e

  3. d

  4. false

Chapter 2 Review (page 43)

  1. d

  2. b

  3. b

  4. d

Chapter 3 Review (page 63)

  1. e

  2. a

  3. d

  4. c

Chapter 4 Review (page 75)

  1. false

  2. true

  3. e

  4. a

Chapter 5 Review (page 88)

  1. a, b, c, d

  2. b, c

  3. a, b, c

  4. false

Chapter 6 Review (page 102)

  1. false

  2. d

  3. c

  4. false

Chapter 7 Review (page 115)

  1. c

  2. d

  3. a

  4. c

Chapter 8 Review (page 123)

  1. false

  2. b

  3. d

  4. true

Glossary

active learning—occurs when students' minds and bodies are engaged in the learning process

Attribute Listing Method—a technique for generating new ideas that can be used with a brainstorming session

authentic learning—real learning that can be measured

Bloom's Taxonomy—a list developed by Benjamin Bloom that categorizes learning skills— knowledge, comprehension, application, analysis, synthesis, and evaluation.

brainstorming—a technique that uses spontaneous creativity to generate ideas

brainwriting—a technique that involves circulating sheets of paper from person to person to generate ideas

cognitive domain—the area of the mind where thinking takes place

complexity—examining themes, issues, problems, and ideas; looking at issues using different perspectives, connecting concepts, integrating in an interdisciplinary way that connects and bridges the curriculum with the goal of enhancing and enriching ideas

content—the processes and knowledge that students learn in school

creative dramatics—a learning tool that uses open-ended ideas and higher-level thinking to synthesize story lines and create dialogue through movement

creativity—the process and ability to create

curiosity—a level of Williams' Taxonomy of Creative Thought in which a learner wants to know more about a topic or idea

differentiation—the strategies, lessons, and methods a teacher uses to meet the needs of the diverse student population through content, process, and product

elaboration—a level of Williams' Taxonomy of Creative Thought that provides more information on a topic

electronic brainstorming—a brainstorming technique used without constraints of time or place through voice messaging, email, and Internet chat rooms

flexibility—a level of Williams' Taxonomy of Creative Thought that encourages modification or the ability to adjust

fluency—a level of Williams' Taxonomy of Creative Thought that encourages fluent ideas

graphic organizer—visual representations of information, which help us gather and sort pertinent information

imagination—a level of Williams' Taxonomy of Creative Thought that encourages imagination and visualization

intrapersonal—the ability to understand one's own feelings and motivations

interpersonal—the ability to understand the feelings and intentions of others

kinesthetic—the ability to use movement for learning

lateral thinking—seeking solutions to problems through unconventional methods, such as brainstorming

learning style—a method of learning that works best and is preferred by an individual

logical/mathematical intelligence—involves reasoning deductively and thinking logically

Morphological Synthesis—attribute listing in a matrix form

Multiple Intelligences Theory—a theory that states all people possess at least eight different kinds of intelligences—verbal/linguistic, logical/mathematical, visual/spatial, bodily/kinesthetic, musical/rhythmic, interpersonal, intrapersonal, and naturalistic

musical/rhythmic intelligence—the ability to recognize and compose musical tones, rhythms, and pitches

naturalistic intelligence—the ability to classify natural phenomena and have an ongoing curiosity and knowledge of the natural world

originality—a level of Williams' Taxonomy of Creative Thought that encourages novel ideas

passive learners—students who take in information through lectures or reading

primary sources—authentic documents, photographs, or items that tell about a time period, person, or place

problem-based learning—a curriculum development and instructional system that simultaneously develops both problem-solving strategies and disciplinary knowledge bases and skills by placing students in the active role of problem solvers confronted with an ill-structured problem that mirrors real-world problems

problem statement—an identification of a problem that is investigated during a problem-based learning activity

reverse brainstorming—brainstorming where new viewpoints are discovered by turning around the basic problem

risk taking—a level of Williams' Taxonomy of Creative Thought in which students are encouraged to take risks in their thinking

SCAMPER—an acronym that is a short version of Alex Osborn's 73 idea-spurring questions—**S** is for substitute, **C** is for combine, **A** is for adapt, **M** is for modify, **P** is for put to other uses, **E** is for eliminate or elaborate, and **R** is for reverse or rearrange

semantic memories—memories that have meaning or connection to prior knowledge

simulations—an active-learning strategy that gets students' minds engaged in the learning at hand

Socratic Seminar—a questioning activity named for Socrates; it is teacher-led and uses open-ended questions to help students analyze a document, photograph, idea, or event

thinking skills—the categories of thinking as described by Bloom

Three Story Intellect Model—a model of questioning that categorizes thinking into three levels—gathering, processing, and applying

vertical thinking—thinking that occurs when one solves a problem by going from one logical step to another logical step

visual learners—those who learn best by seeing pictures, diagrams, or any other visual medium

visual/spatial intelligence—the ability to create mental images and pictures in order to solve problems

Williams' Taxonomy—a list that has eight levels of questions that expand student creativity through the cognitive and affective domains; all eight levels are an extension of synthesizing

References

Barell, J. (2002a). *Problem-based learning: An inquiry approach.* Arlington Heights, IL: Skylight Professional Development.

Barell, J. (2002b). *Teaching for thoughtfulness: Classroom strategies to enhance intellectual development.* Arlington Heights, IL: Skylight Professional Development.

Barell, J. (2003). *Developing more curious minds.* Alexandria, VA: Association for Supervision and Curriculum Development.

Bellanca, J. (2002). *The best of Skylight: Essential teaching tools.* Arlington Heights, IL: Skylight Professional Development.

Bloom, B. S., Englehart, M. D., Furst, E. J., Hill, W. H., & Krathwohl, D. R. (1956). *Taxonomy of educational objectives: The classification of educational goals.* New York: McKay.

Caine, G., & Caine, R. (1997). *Education on the edge of possibility.* Alexandria, VA: Association for Supervision and Curriculum Development.

Campbell, B., & Campbell, L. (1999). *Multiple intelligences and student achievement.* Alexandria, VA: Association for Supervision and Curriculum Development.

Conklin, W. (2003). *Exploring history through primary sources: The Great Depression.* Huntington Beach, CA: Teacher Created Materials.

Crawford, R. (1954). *The techniques of creative thinking.* Portland, OR: Hawthorne Books.

Davis, G. A. (1998). *Creativity is forever.* Dubuque, IA: Kendall/Hunt.

Davis, G. A., Helfert, C. J., & Shapiro, G. R. (1973). Let's be an ice machine!: Creative dramatics. *Spotlight Journal of Creative Behavior, 7,* 37–48.

De Bono, E. (1970). *Lateral thinking: Creativity step by step.* New York: Harper & Row.

Diamond, M., & Hopson, J. (1998). *Magic trees of the mind: How to nurture your child's intelligence, creativity, and healthy emotions from birth through adolescence.* New York: Dutton.

Finkle, S. L., & Torp, L. L. (1995). *Introductory documents.* Aurora, IL: Center for Problem-Based Learning.

Gardner, H. (1993). *Frames of mind: The theory of multiple intelligences.* New York: Basic Books.

Glenn, R. (2002). Brain research. *Teaching for Excellence, 6,* 1–2.

Gourgey, A. (1984, April). *The impact of an improvisational dramatics program on school attitude and achievement.* Paper Presented at the 68th Annual Meeting of the American Educational Research Association, New Orleans, LA.

Hoetker, J. (1969). *Dramatics and the teaching of literature.* Champaign, IL: National Council of Teachers of English/ERIC Clearinghouse on the Teaching of English. (ERIC Document Reproduction Service No. ED028165)

Jensen, E. (1998). *Teaching with the brain in mind.* Alexandria, VA: Association for Supervision and Curriculum Development.

LeDoux, J. (1996). *The emotional brain: The mysterious underpinnings of emotional life.* New York: Simon & Schuster.

McGaugh, J. L., Cahill, L., Parent, M. B., Mesches, M. H., Coleman-Mesches, K., & Salinas, J. A. (1995). Involvement of the amygdala in the regulation of memory storage. In J. L. McGaugh, F. Bermudez-Ratton, & R. A. Prado-Alcala (Eds.), *Plasticity in the central nervous system: Learning and memory* (pp. 17–39). Mahwah, NJ: Lawrence Erlbaum.

Olsen, K. (1995). *Science continuum of concepts for grades K–6.* Federal Way, WA: Books for Educators.

Osborn, A. F. (1953). *Applied imagination.* New York: Scribner's.

Pellegrini, A., & Galda, L. (1982). The effects of thematic fantasy play training on the development of children's story comprehension. *American Educational Research Spotlight Journal, 19,* 443–452.

Sprenger, M. (1999). *Learning and memory: The brain in action.* Alexandria, VA: Association for Supervision and Curriculum Development.

Stix, A. (2004). *Social studies strategies for active learning.* Huntington Beach, CA: Shell Education.

Stix, A., & Hrbek, F. (2000). *Exploring history: The age of exploration.* Huntington Beach, CA: Teacher Created Materials.

Stix, A., & Hrbek, F. (2001a). *Exploring history: Colonial America.* Huntington Beach, CA: Teacher Created Materials.

Stix, A., & Hrbek, F. (2001b). *Exploring history: The Constitution and a new government.* Huntington Beach, CA: Teacher Created Materials.

Stix, A., & Hrbek, F. (2004). *Exploring history: Ancient Egypt.* Huntington Beach, CA: Teacher Created Materials.

Successful strategies for reading in the content areas: Grades 3–5. (2004). Huntington Beach, CA: Shell Education.

Taylor, T. R. Curriculum design for excellene website: http://www.rogertaylor.com.

Teele, S. (1994). *Redesigning the educational system to enable all students to succeed.* Unpublished doctoral dissertation, University of California, Riverside.

Tyler, R. (1949). *Basic principles of curriculum and instruction.* University of Chicago Press.

Wagner, B. J. (1987). *The effect of role playing on the written persuasion of fourth and eighth graders.* ERIC Clearinghouse on Reading and Comprehension. (ERIC Document Reproduction Service No. ED285155)

Way, B. (1967). *Development through drama.* Atlantic Highlands, NJ: Humanities Press.